Science Quest

未来科学への誘い

Seisuke Yasunami

Richard S. Lavin

Photographs by

©iStockphoto.com

音声ファイルのダウンロード／ストリーミング

CDマーク表示がある箇所は、音声を弊社HPより無料でダウンロード／ストリーミングすることができます。トップページのバナーをクリックし、書籍検索してください。書籍詳細ページに音声ダウンロードアイコンがございますのでそちらから自習用音声としてご活用ください。

https://www.seibido.co.jp

Science Quest

はしがき

私たちが生活している地球は様々な課題をかかえていますが、人間の英知を集めれば決して解決できないものはないと考えられます。人為的な行為による大気中の二酸化炭素などの温室効果ガスによって気温が上昇傾向にあり、二酸化炭素の排出を抑えるために具体的な対策が国連を中心とした国際会議で各国政府に求められています。また、情報通信技術の発展によって私たちの生活は劇的に便利になろうとしています。さらに、地球外に目を向けると、宇宙開発にも新たな様々なプロジェクトが計画されています。

本書Science Quest（『未来科学への誘い』）の英文は、私たちを取り巻く現代的で近未来の科学分野に焦点をあてて、大学生向けに中級総合英語教材として書き下ろされたものです。各ユニットの英文の語数は450語程度、辞書に頼ることなく読み、内容を理解できるようにしています。ユニット内の指示文は英語で書いていますが、Pre-reading、While-reading、Post-readingの各段階で、英単語と定義文による語彙確認、リーディング、英語の質問に対して英文で答える内容把握、英語による大意把握、TOEIC®試験形式による英語表現の確認、英語表現、トピックと関連した会話の部分聞き取り、さらに、グラフや表を用いた英語によるディスカッションタスクを課しています。つまり、英語の「読み」「書き」「聞き」「話す」という4技能が総合的に学習できます。

本書のトピックは、ニュースやTV番組でしばしば取り上げられるものですが、理系の学生だけでなく文系の学生にも興味を持って接することができます。次の4つの観点からWORLDを見つめています。 THE LIVING WORLDでは、動物や生態系などの知られざる営みに触れることができます。THE NATURAL WORLDでは、エネルギーや環境と人間の関わりに関する問題に迫ることができます。THE TECHNOLOGICAL WORLDでは、情報技術の発展と人間の生活の変化への対応が述べられています。THE WORLD BEYONDでは、遥かかなたの宇宙開発などに視野を向けさせてくれます。

本書を通して、我々人類が直面している問題を再確認して理解を深めることは、学生の皆さんの将来にとって有意義であると確信しています。また、取り上げられたトピックや関連事項について、ネットなどで調べられることもお薦めします。情報を発信するにはしっかりとした知識と問題意識を持って英語に接するようにしてください。

最後になりますが、本書の出版をお勧め頂いた成美堂社長佐野英一郎氏、編集部の佐野泰孝氏、小亀正人氏には大変お世話になりました。心からの感謝を申し上げます。

安浪　誠祐
Richard S. Lavin

本書の使い方

Vocabulary Preview

本文に使用される重要な語句に焦点をあて抽出した10語を取り上げています。英語による定義の中から選択して、語彙を確認してください。できるだけ辞書に頼らずに解答しますが、最後には必ず辞書で確認してください。

Reading

本文は科学分野のトピックですが、必ずしも専門分野の知識を必要としません。できるだけ平易で分かり易い英語で書かれています。黙読、音読、音声を聞く、音声を聞きながら音読などの活動をお勧めします。

Notes

難しい語句や固有名詞などの意味を説明しています。必要に応じて参考にしてください。

Comprehension Check

本文の内容を正確に理解したかどうかを確認するための質問です。質問に対する答えとして最も適当なものを(a)〜(c)から選んでください。

Best Summary

本文の内容を要約した英文として最も適当なものを4つの選択肢から選んでください。

Word Choice

TOEIC®試験形式の問題で、英文の空所に最も適当な語句を4つの選択肢から選んでください。語句は本文に出てきたものです。

Composition

日本語の意味を表すように(　　　　)の語句を適当に並べ替えてください。文頭に来る語は大文字にしてください。表現は本文に出てきたものです。

Partial Dictation and Conversation

本文と関連したトピックのダイアローグになっています。空欄に聞き取った英語を入れて、ペアになってダイアローグの練習を行ってください。

Active Learning

グラフや表を見て、3つの質問に対するディスカッションを自由に行います。その際に、WORDS & PHRASESを参考にしてください。

Contents

THE TECHNOLOGICAL WORLD

THE WORLD BEYOND

UNIT 1

Fast Asleep?

動物たちの眠り

人間と同様にすべての動物に眠りが必要である。群れで暮らす動物、大型の動物、空中を飛び続ける鳥類、半脳が眠る動物などは、生息環境や身体的脅威の有無など自然界の条件によって、どのように睡眠を取っているのだろうか。

Vocabulary Preview

Match each word with a definition by drawing a line between them.

1. eliminate •   • (a) to move without making any special effort

2. species •   • (b) a kind of animal or plant

3. predator •   • (c) to put something inside something else

4. herd •   • (d) to determine, or to find out that something is true

5. drift •   • (e) to change in response to the environment

6. surface •   • (f) very surprising

7. implant •   • (g) the top layer of something

8. ascertain •   • (h) a group of animals such as cows

9. evolve •   • (i) an animal that attacks or is a threat to another

10. astonishing •   • (j) to get rid of; to dispose of

The available evidence suggests that all animals need sleep. In modern civilizations, humans have eliminated most **imminent** physical threats, so we are able to sleep deeply for several hours continuously. Most animals, in contrast, need to balance the need for rest with the need to protect themselves from danger.

5   Different species balance those two needs in interesting ways.

Some animals spend very little time at all asleep. Giraffes in the wild have been calculated to spend roughly eight percent of their day asleep. They sometimes lie down, resting their head on their **rump**. To avoid being caught by predators, they do this for only a few minutes at a time. Often, though, they nap while standing up,

10   which allows them to get moving more quickly at any sign of danger. Horses also exhibit the same behavior. One advantage of living in a herd, as horses and giraffes do, is that some animals can sleep while others stay awake to watch out for danger.

Another animal that sleeps for only a very small portion of the day is the **sperm whale**. Before sleeping, sperm whales dive down **headfirst** a short distance, then

15   passively drift head up to the surface. Researchers say that they do not move or even breathe while sleeping, but that they wake up after 10 to 15 minutes. Sperm whales sleep even less than giraffes, about seven percent of each day. Researchers discovered this behavior only in 2008, and it was caught on camera in 2017.

Researchers know very little about the sleeping habits of birds, but in 2016, by

20   implanting sensors in **frigatebirds'** skulls, they were able to ascertain that the birds are able to take naps of only about 10 seconds while flying. This enables them to get enough rest to remain **airborne** for long stretches of time, up to two months. Since frigatebirds are unable to swim, or even float in water, this ability is essential when they are crossing the sea.

25   Some animals, such as **bottlenose dolphins**, use **unihemispheric** sleep, where only half of the brain is asleep at any one time. This allows the dolphins to control their breathing so that they breathe in the air that they need when they come to the surface while still getting rest. After a certain amount of time, the hemisphere that was asleep wakes up and the other hemisphere has a period of sleep.

30   Some of what scientists know about sleep has been discovered only in the last decade, suggesting that there are sleep behaviors that are as yet unknown. What we

do know indicates that animals have evolved an astonishing array of mechanisms to ensure that they can get the rest they need while protecting themselves from danger.

NOTES

imminent 差し迫った **rump** 臀部 **sperm whale** マッコウクジラ **headfirst** 頭から先に **frigatebird** グンカンドリ **airborne** 飛行して **bottlenose dolphin** バンドウイルカ **unihemispheric** 半脳の

Comprehension Check

Choose the most suitable answer for each question.

1. Why are humans able to sleep deeply and continuously?
   (a) We are able to balance threats against each other.
   (b) Our large brains need more rest.
   (c) We usually don't need to worry about physical threats.

2. Why do horses often nap while standing up?
   (a) They can respond more quickly to danger.
   (b) Lying down is uncomfortable.
   (c) Their herd pressures them to stand up.

3. How did researchers find out that some birds nap while flying?
   (a) They watched the birds closely when they were flying low.
   (b) They attached instruments to their wings.
   (c) They put sensors in their skulls.

4. What is unihemispheric sleep?
   (a) It is a pattern of sleep whereby animals such as dolphins in the southern hemisphere sleep one night and dolphins in the northern hemisphere sleep the next night.
   (b) It is a pattern of sleep in animals such as dolphins whereby only one half of the brain is asleep for a time, and then the other half.
   (c) It is a pattern of sleep in animals such as dolphins whereby only one half of the brain needs sleep and the other is always awake.

Best Summary

From these four sentences, choose the one that summarizes the passage best.

1. Unlike humans, most animals face environmental threats, so they use a variety of ways to get rest while avoiding being left unprotected for a long time.

2. Most animals avoid lying down to sleep, because it would take too long to stand up and run away from danger.

3. It has proved difficult for scientists to study the large variety of animals on the planet; accordingly, little is known about the sleep habits of most of them.

4. To avoid being attacked, most animals probably do not sleep at all.

Word Choice

Choose a suitable expression to fill each blank.

1. Sperm whales sleep for _____ seven percent of each day.
   (a) roughly   (b) approximate   (c) exactly   (d) in the range

2. Giraffes tend to run at the first _____ of danger.
   (a) signal   (b) indicate   (c) sign   (d) cue

3. For optimal efficiency, humans need to _____ that they get sufficient sleep.
   (a) assure   (b) ensure   (c) ascertain   (d) claim

4. Some birds can swim well, but others are _____ do so.
   (a) disable of   (b) incapable to   (c) unable to   (d) disabled to

5. Outside of our comfortable, advanced societies, humans often _____ the same instincts as animals.
   (a) disturb   (b) exhibit   (c) allow   (d) prevail

Composition

Rearrange the words within the parentheses to make sentences.

1. 平均的な成人の理想的な睡眠時間は7、8時間と計算されている。
   The ideal sleeping time for the average adult human (be / been / calculated / eight / has / seven / to / to) hours.

2. グンカンドリは海に落ちるのを避けるために極めて短時間の仮眠を取る。

   Frigatebirds (avoid / extremely / falling / naps / short / take / to) into the sea.

   _____

3. 立ったまま眠る主な利点は捕食動物が近付いたら動物たちが逃げられることである。

   The (advantage / main / of / sleeping / standing / while) is that it allows animals to run away if a predator approaches.

   _____

4. 眠るために横になることの問題点は、動物たちが、捕食動物から逃れるために、逃げ出したり立ち上がることさえできないかもしれないことである。

   The problem with lying down to sleep is that animals may not be able to (away / even / in / or / run / stand / time / up) to escape a predator.

   _____

Partial Dictation and Conversation 🔊 1-08

Listen to the dialogue, and fill in the missing words. Then, speak the dialogue with a partner. After speaking once or twice, switch roles.

A: Your dog looks so cute asleep. Oh, sorry, it looks like I

⃞1 _____ .

B: Like most animals, he sleeps very lightly. If he hears another dog, or a cat,

⃞2 _____ , he tends to wake up right away.

A: I wonder why that is.

B: Well, you have to remember that, in the wild, those sounds

⃞3 _____ represent danger. After all, on an evolutionary scale, it isn't so long ago that all dogs were wild.

A: I guess you ⃞4 _____ there. By the way, have you seen a horse lie down to sleep?

B: Yes. A horse sometimes lies down to sleep. Other times, it will sleep

⃞5 _____ .

Look at the graph below, which shows the sleep time ranges according to age recommended by the U.S.'s *National Sleep Foundation*. With a partner, talk about these recommendations and your sleep habits, including the following questions.

1. How do people's sleep requirements change with age?

2. How do these times compare to the amount of sleep you usually get now?

3. Do you think the recommendations are reasonable?

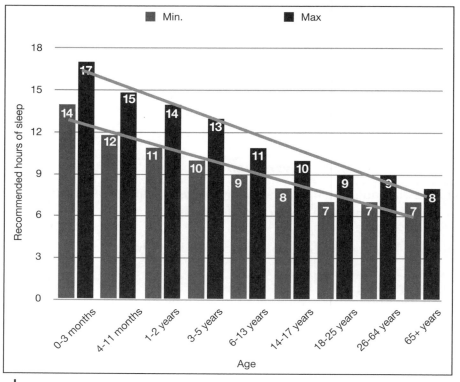

[Data source: https://www.sleepfoundation.org/articles/how-much-sleep-do-we-really-need]

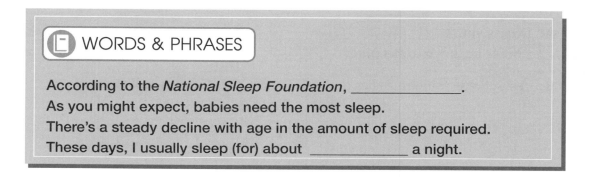

WORDS & PHRASES

According to the *National Sleep Foundation*, _____.
As you might expect, babies need the most sleep.
There's a steady decline with age in the amount of sleep required.
These days, I usually sleep (for) about _____ a night.

UNIT 2 All Gone?

種消滅の危機

種の絶滅には人間が直接的な原因ではないものもあるが、人間が経済的発展を優先する行動によって失われている種の数も多い。種の多様性を維持するために人間はどのようにすべきだろうか。

Vocabulary Preview

Match each word with a definition by drawing a line between them.

1. extinct
2. majority
3. catastrophe
4. ongoing
5. biodiversity
6. biosphere
7. conserve
8. ratio
9. aware
10. fault

- (a) more than half
- (b) the part of the world in which life can exist
- (c) no longer existing
- (d) a violent change or disaster
- (e) a state in which there are many different forms of life
- (f) knowing or being conscious of something
- (g) continuing
- (h) a relationship between two numbers
- (i) responsibility for failure or for doing something wrong
- (j) to keep in a safe state

It is estimated that anything from 200 to 100,000 species become extinct every year. The lack of precision is due to the fact that we do not know how many species actually exist. Extinction is part of the natural world, so it is reasonable to ask why we should care about species that are in danger of extinction. **Ecologists** tell us that the current rate of species loss is probably at least 1,000 times faster than the natural extinction rate, i.e. the rate at which species would become extinct if it were not for the influence of humans. The mass extinctions from history — such as the **Cretaceous-Paleogene** extinction event 66 million years ago, which wiped out most of the dinosaurs and indeed a majority of all species on the Earth — are thought to have been triggered by short-term catastrophes such as sea-level falls or **asteroid** impacts, after which the environment could recover. In contrast, the current crisis is ongoing, and without **deliberate** action by humans there is no reason to think it will **abate**. Indeed, some scientists think that we might lose a third of all species by the middle of this century.

Apart from an **instinctive** sadness we might feel at the loss of a familiar species such as the giant panda, the Asian elephant, the tiger, or the orangutan, a key reason to focus efforts on conservation is to maintain biodiversity. Different species perform different roles in the **ecosystem** that may not be fully understood. When a species disappears, that **unleashes** a chain of events that may not be **predictable**. A well-known example is honeybees. As their number has decreased, there have been **strains** on agriculture. If honeybees disappear, it is likely that some plants that depend on them for **pollination** will also become extinct.

Some scientists have attempted to **quantify** the costs of biodiversity loss and the benefits of maintenance of the biosphere in economic terms in order to **incentivize** action to conserve species. A 1997 study found that, whereas the global economy at the time was valued at $18 trillion a year, the biosphere provided services worth around $33 trillion a year. A follow-up study showed that the benefits of conserving biodiversity would exceed the costs by a ratio of about 100 to one.

Why, then, more than 20 years after the 1997 study, has species loss not been slowed? Ignorance no doubt plays a role. More fundamentally, though, whereas benefits of conservation are generally long-term and serve everyone, the short-term gains for specific people, organizations, or communities of continuing activities that threaten species may be very great. Some suggest that **conventional** economic models, **devised** at a time when people were not fully aware of environmental threats, are at fault. New economic models should take into account the ecological costs and benefits of our actions.

35

NOTES

ecologist 生態学者　**Cretaceous-Paleogene** 白亜紀－古第三紀　**asteroid** 小惑星
deliberate 熟考した上での　**abate** 和らぐ　**instinctive** 直感的な　**ecosystem** 生態系
unleash 〜を解き放つ　**predictable** 予測できる　**strain** ひずみ　**pollination** 受粉
quantify 〜を数値で表す　**incentivize** 奨励する　**conventional** 従来の
devise 〜を考案する

Comprehension Check

Choose the most suitable answer for each question.

1. What is the difference between species loss now and mass extinctions from history?
   (a) There are no dinosaurs now.
   (b) Historical mass extinctions were triggered by short-term catastrophes, whereas there is a risk that current species loss could continue indefinitely.
   (c) Species loss was faster in the past.

2. Why is biodiversity important?
   (a) For their healthy operation, ecosystems require different species to perform various functions.
   (b) Without biodiversity, pollination will not occur.
   (c) When biodiversity is lost, we feel very sad.

3. What is the economic rationale for protecting biodiversity?
   (a) The services provided by a diverse biosphere are very valuable.
   (b) Without doing so, it will be difficult to grow the economy beyond about $33 trillion.
   (c) Although the costs of doing so are very high, we should do it because wildlife gives us great pleasure.

4. What is NOT said about economic models?
   (a) They should include ecological costs and benefits.
   (b) Current ones reflect insufficient awareness of environmental threats.
   (c) We should not blame economists for them.

Best Summary

From these four sentences, choose the one that summarizes the passage best.

1. Because of the difficulty of researching animals, scientists are not at all confident how many species actually exist.

2. Since extinction is a natural process that cannot be changed, it is not appropriate for humans to worry about it.

3. The number of species lost to human activity is so large that it is important for us to take urgent action to slow the rate of loss.

4. Although all species are important, it is particularly important to protect large animals such as the giant panda and the Asian elephant.

Word Choice

Choose a suitable expression to fill each blank.

1. What will happen if the number of species continues to decrease rapidly is
   _____.
   (a) optimistic   (b) impactful   (c) unpredictable   (d) expectant

2. It is difficult to _____ the benefits of healthy ecosystems.
   (a) quantize   (b) quantify   (c) be value   (d) qualification

3. Many species are _____ disappearing altogether.
   (a) in danger of   (b) in risk of   (c) dangerous   (d) risky

4. A scientific explanation attempts to take all the facts _____.
   (a) reckoned   (b) accounted   (c) to consideration (d) into account

5. The northern blue whale is considered to be "of least concern"; _____, the Beluga whale is classified as "critically endangered."
   (a) by comparison (b) contrasting   (c) in contrast   (d) in comparison

Composition

Rearrange the words within the parentheses to make sentences.

1. これまで100年間にわたって人間の人口が急激に増加していなければ、種の消失はもっと緩やかかもしれない。
   Species loss might be much (for / if / it / not / rapid / slower / the / were) rise in the human population over the last 100 years.

2. 私たちが自然を尊重できなかったことを考慮するときに、近代経済学に責任があると多くの学者たちが言う。

When considering our failure to value nature, many (at / economics / fault / is / modern / say / scholars / that).

_____

3. いくつかの短期的な犠牲を払う必要があるという事実のために、絶滅危惧種を救うのは難しい。

It is difficult to save endangered species (due / fact / it / requires / that / the / to) us to make some short-term sacrifices.

_____

4. ジャワトラは既に絶滅していて、アモイトラは野生では絶滅しているが、ベンガルトラを救う可能性はまだある。

(already / and / extinct / is / Javan / the / tiger / whereas) the South China tiger is extinct in the wild, there is still a chance of saving the Bengal tiger.

_____

Partial Dictation and Conversation

1-13

Listen to the dialogue, and fill in the missing words. Then, speak the dialogue with a partner. After speaking once or twice, switch roles.

A: Those pandas sure don't look very energetic.

B: Well, ⨂1 _____ living their whole lives in this small enclosure, so I guess they get bored. In any case, pandas eat mainly bamboo shoots, which ⨂2 _____ so much nutrition, so they have sedentary lifestyles.

A: I heard it's really expensive ⨂3 _____. Don't they eat a lot of bamboo shoots?

B: That's right. I heard it was ⨂4 _____ 10 kilograms a day.

A: Oh, yes, and aren't they very fussy? I saw on TV that they throw away bamboo shoots ⨂5 _____.

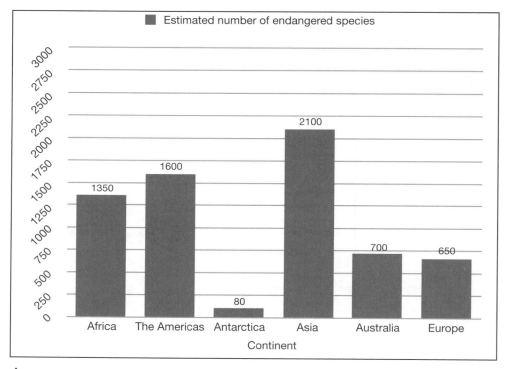

Active Learning

Look at the graph below, which shows the estimated number of endangered species in six areas. Talk about the data with a partner, including the following questions.

1. About how many endangered species are there estimated to be altogether?

2. Where are most of the endangered species concentrated? Why might that be?

3. Which continent has the smallest number of endangered species? Why might that be?

[Data source: https://caitlynkeable.wordpress.com/2013/04/10/number-of-endangered-species-per-continent/]

🗐 WORDS & PHRASES

The number of endangered species _____.

The continent with the largest number of endangered species _____.

_____ and _____ also have a large number of _____.

The reason why _____ has (have) a large number of endangered species is that _____.

UNIT 3

Beeing and Nothingness

ミツバチがいなくなったら

ミツバチは蜂蜜を人間に提供したり、農作物の受粉に大いに役立つが、最近、ミツバチやミツバチのコロニーが、寄生虫や殺虫剤などのさまざまな理由で姿を消す現象が確認されている。その実態を詳しく読んでみよう。

Vocabulary Preview

Match each word with a definition by drawing a line between them.

1. mead   •   • (a) a structure in which bees live

2. hive   •   • (b) a chemical used to kill small organisms that harm crops

3. coin   •   • (c) to invent a new word or expression

4. collapse   •   • (d) an alcoholic drink made of honey, water, and yeast

5. parasite   •   • (e) a great tiredness or exhaustion

6. originate   •   • (f) a smell

7. habitat   •   • (g) an animal or plant that lives in or on another animal or plant

8. pesticide   •   • (h) to start or come from

9. fatigue   •   • (i) the natural home of a living thing

10. scent   •   • (j) a sudden failure in the functioning of something

In ancient times, honey was the most important **sweetener** for alcoholic drinks such as mead and for food. Although humankind now has access to sugar from **sugarcane** and many other sweeteners, honey is still prized as a sweetener. Bees, though, are important for much more than their ability to create this prized product.

5   Bees and other insects, along with bats and birds, can **pollinate** many plants. But modern large-scale agriculture depends on professionally managed honeybee hives, which can improve the quality of the crop and maximize **yield**. Many farmers rent the services of professional beekeepers, who travel long distances with their hives to have their bees ready to pollinate a crop during its flowering season. In
10   recent years, beekeepers have been complaining about massive losses in colonies, and researchers have coined the term "**colony collapse disorder.**"

Scientists and beekeepers have pointed to a number of possible reasons for this phenomenon. One is parasites such as the **Varroa mite**, which originated in Asia and then spread throughout the world. Bees in Europe and North America have no
15   resistance to the mite, which has no natural predators and can destroy a colony in a very short time. Others are habitat loss and lack of a varied food supply. Bees get their necessary **nutrients** from a variety of plants, including wild flowers. If land is cleared for building or for agriculture, their food supply disappears or becomes less varied, leading to health problems or death. Bees also suffer from extreme heat
20   or cold, meaning that the unpredictable weather resulting from climate change can **take its toll**. The fall season often leads to massive losses of colonies.

A major **contributor** to bee deaths and colony loss in recent years is agricultural pesticides, especially **neonicotinoids**. In high doses, these cause acute poisoning and death; in **low doses**, they appear to **compromise** bees' ability to navigate,
25   resulting in them being unable to find their way back to the hive after **foraging**. It is interesting to note that one study found **residues** of more than 150 different pesticides in beehives. Each pesticide alone, and in combination with others, may have effects that are as yet not fully understood. It is also important not to forget that these pesticides will to some degree be present in any honey collected from these
30   hives.

Studies have suggested that being overworked can lead to fatigue in bees, reducing their ability to recognize new scents. This ability is **crucial** when they are introduced to new crops. This results in a **vicious cycle** whereby the other factors listed here lead to smaller numbers of bees being available, and these bees thus become overworked, leading in turn to more bee deaths and colony collapse. 35

> **NOTES**
>
> **sweetener** 甘味料　**sugarcane** サトウキビ　**pollinate** 〜に受粉する　**yield** 収穫高
> **colony collapse disorder** 蜂群崩壊症候群　**Varroa mite** ミツバチヘギイタダニ　**nutrient**
> 栄養分　**take one's toll** 大きな悪影響を及ぼす　**contributor** 要因　**neonicotinoid** ネオニ
> コチノイド　**low dose** 低用量　**compromise** 〜を損なう　**foraging** 食糧探し　**residue**
> 残留物　**crucial** 極めて重要な　**vicious cycle** 悪循環

Comprehension Check

Choose the most suitable answer for each question.

1. Which of the following is true?
   (a) Professionally managed bees are too expensive for large-scale agriculture.
   (b) Using honeybees at the right time can maximize crop yields.
   (c) Beekeepers say that it is not possible to improve the quality of crops by using honeybees.

2. How can clearing land for agriculture be a problem for bees?
   (a) When existing flowers and other plants disappear, the bees' diet becomes poorer.
   (b) When the appearance of the land changes, bees lose their ability to navigate.
   (c) Some agricultural crops are poisonous for bees.

3. What is a problem with neonicotinoids?
   (a) They are new, untested products that may not be effective.
   (b) They are safe when used alone but many farmers mix them with other pesticides in dangerous ways.
   (c) Bees ingesting them in low doses may lose their ability to find their way back home.

4. Which of the following is NOT mentioned as a possible cause of colony collapse disorder?
   (a) The Varroa mite
   (b) Overwork
   (c) Mild weather

From these four sentences, choose the one that summarizes the passage best.

1. Because other animals can carry out pollination, bees are now important mainly for the honey that they produce, rather than for their ecological functions.

2. In recent years, a worrying number of bees and bee colonies have been lost for a variety of reasons.

3. Neonicotinoids combine with other pesticides to form a variety of dangerous substances that can harm bees and other insects and disrupt ecosystems.

4. Bees in Europe and North America have no way to defend themselves against the Varroa mite and other parasites.

Word Choice

Choose a suitable expression to fill each blank.

1. A _____ of adequate nutrition can cause disease in bees as in humans
   (a) lack   (b) missing   (c) shortness   (d) inadequacy

2. I need to _____ the services of a beekeeper. Do you know where I can find one?
   (a) loan   (b) lend   (c) lent   (d) rent

3. The effectiveness of some insecticides can be _____ by hot weather.
   (a) complexified   (b) affiliated   (c) compromised   (d) disaffected

4. Colony collapse disorder is a phenomenon _____ many bees die for no obvious reason.
   (a) whereby   (b) throughout   (c) therefore   (d) henceforth

5. For bees, being exposed to neonicotinoids can result in _____ unable to navigate.
   (a) them to be   (b) them being   (c) their been   (d) they are

Composition

Rearrange the words within the parentheses to make sentences.

1. ハチミツの中に含まれる殺虫剤はある程度有害であると想像に難くない。
   It is easy to imagine that the pesticides (are / harmful / honey / in / present / some / to) degree.

2. 私たちの多くが昆虫を不快に感じるが、昆虫が生態系にもたらす多大な貢献を忘れないようにするのは重要である。

Although many of us find insects unpleasant, it (contribution / forget / important / is / massive / not / the / to) they make to ecosystems.

_____

3. 集約農業は開墾を伴うが、結果的に多くの植物や動物が生息地を失うことになる。

Intensive agriculture involves clearing land, (and / animals / in / losing / many / plants / resulting) their habitat.

_____

4. 蜂群崩壊症候群で失われる蜂の数は今のところははっきりしない。

The number of bees (as / colony collapse disorder / is / lost / to / unclear / yet).

_____

Partial Dictation and Conversation

🎧 1-19

Listen to the dialogue, and fill in the missing words. Then, speak the dialogue with a partner. After speaking once or twice, switch roles.

A: Wow, what happened to you? Your face looks rather swollen.

B: I ⟦1⟧ _____ a bee this morning.

A: Oh, no. That must have been painful. What ⟦2⟧ _____ bee was it?

B: What kind of bee?! I don't know. I ⟦3⟧ _____ saw it. And it's still painful now.

A: Well, in that case, it's possible that it wasn't even a bee. It ⟦4⟧ _____ a wasp.

B: Yes, you may be right. Right now, I think the key thing is to find out what it was.

A: Really? Well, why don't you take me to ⟦5⟧ _____ you were stung?

B: No, not really! I don't care what it was! I just want to forget about it!

Active Learning

Look at the chart below, showing the number of bees sighted by members of the *BeeSpotter* network in Illinois, USA. With a partner, talk about what you see in the chart, including the questions below.

1. What is the general pattern over the year?

2. How many bees were spotted in March and how many in July?

3. What foods in our daily lives do you think depend on bees?

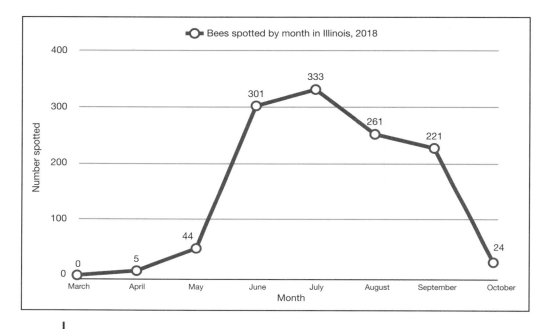

[Data source: https://beespotter.org/]

WORDS & PHRASES

The number of bees sighted increases sharply from _____
and declines sharply from _____.
In March, _____. In July, _____.
I guess that fruits such as _____ are pollinated by bees.

UNIT 4

As Clever as Us?

賢い動物たち

人間だけが知的能力が高いわけではない。人間の基準ではなく一般化された基準を用いて調べてみると、さまざまな動物が人間よりもいかに優れた特別な能力を持っているのかが解明される。

Vocabulary Preview

Match each word with a definition by drawing a line between them.

1. assume   • (a) to create or design something new

2. ability   • (b) made of many connected parts

3. brain   • (c) to think that something is true

4. abstract   • (d) the most basic and important quality of something

5. grief   • (e) the thing in your head that enables you to think

6. compassion   • (f) a feeling of deep sadness

7. complex   • (g) being capable of doing something

8. differentiate   • (h) not concrete

9. invent   • (i) to distinguish between things

10. essence   • (j) a feeling of sympathy for people

Humans have always tended to assume that we are far more intelligent than other animals, although we have long known that dogs, chimpanzees, and dolphins, for example, are clever in various ways. Traditional attempts to test animal intelligence have involved assigning to animals the kinds of tasks that humans
5 would be given in intelligence tests. One scientist's question makes the **absurdity** of such an approach clear: "What if giraffes tested our ability to strip leaves off high tree branches?"

Although it is not possible for us to totally abandon our human **frame of reference**, it is possible to refine our ideas about intelligence and make them more
10 general. A major **indicator** of intelligence appears to be the size, both **absolute** and **relative** to body size, of an animal's brain. In one type of test, scientists check whether an animal realizes that what it sees in the mirror is itself. Another type seeks to establish the animal's ability to remember things and to recognize other animals it has seen (or heard or smelled) before. Scientists also try to ascertain animals' ability
15 to solve problems and to use tools.

The land animal with the largest brain of all is the elephant. One use to which elephants appear to put their brains is remembering things; in particular, their long-term memory is excellent, and they are able to recognize people or other elephants that they haven't seen for many years. Their thinking also appears to have an abstract
20 quality. For example, if they have been harmed by people who speak a particular language, they will tend to avoid people speaking the same language. They also show pain, grief, happiness, and compassion, being similar to humans in several ways.

Moving to the sea, dolphins are well-known for their clever and playful nature,
25 and many readers may have seen dolphin shows in theme parks. Dolphins are able to remember complex sequences as well as differentiate between things that are broadly similar. Psychologists have conducted experiments in which dolphins were given a kind of underwater keyboard to play with. Each key had a different symbol and gave a different kind of treat, as well as **emitting** a different sound. Unlike other
30 animals, the dolphins not only **memorized** the meanings of the different symbols quickly, but also imitated the sounds and combined them to invent new games.

Apes are another type of animal recognized as intelligent. Like dolphins, they seem to have high linguistic abilities, being able to learn sign language and communicate with humans to some extent. In particular, chimpanzees have excellent short-term memory, far better even than humans do.

35

There are many other species of animals that exhibit intelligence of various kinds, among them crows, turtles, **parrots**, and bees. As scientists find out more about how these and other animals think, we are likely to gain a better understanding of the essence of intelligence.

NOTES

absurdity 不合理　**frame of reference** 基準枠　**indicator** 指標　**absolute** 絶対的な
relative 相対的な　**emit** ～を発する　**memorize** ～を記憶する　**parrot** オウム

Comprehension Check

Choose the most suitable answer for each question.

1. What is the significance of the question in lines 6-7: "What if giraffes tested our ability to strip leaves off high tree branches?"
   (a) Intelligence tests need to consider differences between species appropriately.
   (b) Animals are not capable of testing people.
   (c) Giraffes' abilities are very limited.

2. What is the relationship between brain size and intelligence?
   (a) There is no relationship.
   (b) A large brain relative to body size usually signals high intelligence.
   (c) Larger brain sizes, in absolute terms and relative to body size, usually signal high intelligence.

3. Which of the following is NOT mentioned in connection with elephants?
   (a) They show several emotions.
   (b) Their short-term memory is good.
   (c) They seem to be able to distinguish between languages.

4. In experiments, how were dolphins different from other animals?
   (a) They combined sounds in new ways.
   (b) They learned sign language.
   (c) They refused to take part in the experiments.

Best Summary

From these four sentences, choose the one that summarizes the passage best.

1. Intelligence comes in different forms in the animal kingdom, and scientists are gradually learning more about how different animals think.

2. Many animals are intelligent, but dolphins are the most intelligent of all.

3. Many animals can do things that appear intelligent but that, on careful inspection, are just tricks; no animals show real intelligence.

4. When judging animals' intelligence, it is important to make sure that they can perform the kinds of tasks that humans can do.

Word Choice

Choose a suitable expression to fill each blank.

1. Scientists are _____ develop suitable tests to measure animal intelligence.
   (a) looking for   (b) seeking to   (c) hunting to   (d) questing at

2. _____ approach to the question of animal intelligence promises to find new answers and generate new questions.
   (a) Such   (b) Thus   (c) This kind   (d) Such an

3. The whale is thought by some to be the largest animal _____.
   (a) all the world   (b) of all   (c) all in   (d) in existing

4. There are several kinds of bird that are considered to be very intelligent, _____ crows and parrots.
   (a) among them   (b) include   (c) included   (d) altogether

5. In some tasks, chimpanzees _____ much higher ability than most humans.
   (a) exhibit   (b) exude   (c) exclude   (d) excel

Composition

Rearrange the words within the parentheses to make sentences.

1. 私たちは、今後数年で、ますます動物の知能について発見する可能性が高い。
   We (about / and / are / discover / likely / more / more / to) animal intelligence in the coming years.

2. 象は記憶力が優れているだけでなく抽象的に考えることができるということで注目に値する。

Elephants are notable in that they are capable (abstract / as / as / great / having / of / thought / well) memories.

_____

3. イルカは音を真似るだけでなくそれらをある程度創造的に組み合わせることもできる。

Dolphins are able not (also / but / combine / imitate / only / sounds / to / to) them creatively to some extent.

_____

4. 類人猿は知られている動物の中で最も知的であるようだと、多くの科学者たちが言う。

Many scientists say that the great ape (animal / appears / be / intelligent / known / most / the / to).

_____

Partial Dictation and Conversation

🎧 1-26

Listen to the dialogue, and fill in the missing words. Then, speak the dialogue with a partner. After speaking once or twice, switch roles.

A: Hey, ① _____ you went to Thailand. How was it?

B: It was great. I spent ② _____ in the northern part of the country. I took a boat ride, rode a buffalo, and watched an elephant show.

A: An elephant show?

B: Yes. ③ _____. The elephants did some dancing, and one elephant ④ _____.

A: That sounds interesting. I heard that elephants are very intelligent.

B: Yes, ⑤ _____. Apparently, they have really good memories.

Look at the chart below, which shows the *encephalization quotient* (EQ, a rough measure of the brain size of a species compared to the expected brain size based on the body size of the species) and actual brain weight. Both of these have been considered to be indicators of the likely intelligence of a species. Talk about what you see with a partner, including the questions below. (Note that different sources give different figures and that there is a lot of variation between individuals.)

1. Of the animals shown, which animals have especially high and especially low brain weights?

2. Of the animals shown, which animals have especially high and especially low EQs?

3. What does the graph tell us about dogs? Does that match your impression?

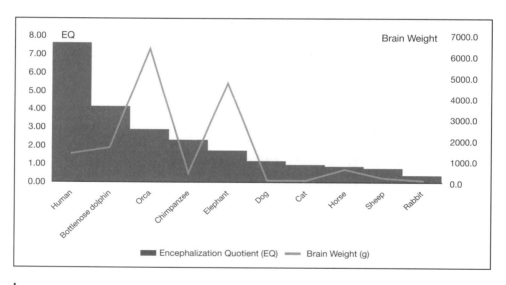

[Data sources: https://en.wikipedia.org/wiki/Brain-to-body_mass_ratio
https://faculty.washington.edu/chudler/facts.html]

WORDS & PHRASES

Orcas and elephants have _____.
Humans and bottlenose dolphins have _____.
The EQ and brain weight are not high. And/But _____.

Life in the Oceans

海洋の生態系

地球上の陸地で詳しく調査されていないところもあるが、海はさらに未知の世界である。海にはさまざまな生き物がいて多様性に富んでいるが、これまで維持されてきた生態系が人間の活動によって危機的な状況におかれている。

Vocabulary Preview

Match each word with a definition by drawing a line between them.

1. speculate •

2. microbe •

3. photosynthesis •

4. mammal •

5. numerous •

6. defecate •

7. sludge •

8. acidification •

9. dissolve •

10. alkaline •

• (a) an extremely small living thing

• (b) a kind of animal where an adult female feeds the young with milk from her own body

• (c) to send out solid waste from one's body

• (d) a soft, thick mud

• (e) a process whereby the pH value of a substance goes down

• (f) (of a liquid) to take in a gas or solid so that it is incorporated

• (g) with a pH of greater than seven

• (h) a process whereby plants turn carbon dioxide and water into food using sunlight

• (i) to consider what the truth might be or what might happen

• (j) many

Although there are corners of the land area of the Earth that have not been explored, the real unknown kingdom is the ocean. Oceans cover nearly three-quarters of the Earth's surface, and scientists say that less than five percent of the oceans has been explored. Life on the Earth began in the oceans more than 600
5 million years ago, and today around 230,000 known species live there. But so much about them remains unknown that researchers speculate that the total number of species living there may be more than two million.

Most of the life in the oceans — around 70 percent — consists of **microorganisms**, which are by definition **invisible** to the naked eye. Marine microbes play a key role
10 in photosynthesis and in driving all global ecosystems. Going up in size, there are countless **marine algae**, plants, **fungi**, **worms**, and **molluscs**. And of course there are many kinds of fish. Of particular interest are marine mammals, which include some of the most intelligent species on the planet. Marine mammals include whales, dolphins, **sea lions**, **sea otters**, **seals**, and **polar bears**.

15 Marine mammals appear to play very important environmental roles. Sea otters, although not particularly numerous, eat **sea urchins**, keeping their **population** in check. Sea urchins eat **kelp**, so the presence of too many sea urchins often leads to ecosystem collapse as other **organisms** that depend on kelp lose their habitat or main source of nutrition. Whales also appear to play a very important role: by
20 swimming to the surface to defecate, they carry **nitrogen** from deep in the ocean to the surface.

The oceans are **beset** by a number of serious environmental challenges. These threaten all kinds of marine life, but marine mammals are under particular threat, because they tend to live in exactly the places where humans' impact on the ocean
25 environment is greatest.

Trash, especially plastic, is one of the greatest of these environmental threats. Most plastic is **non-biodegradable**, so, without specific action to get rid of it, it simply continues to **accumulate** in the oceans. The plastic is mixed with chemical sludge, and much of it has broken into small particles suspended in the water. In many
30 cases, it is mistaken for food by marine species and thus enters the **food chain**.

Another issue that concerns scientists is ocean acidification. The oceans are estimated to dissolve more than 30 percent of the carbon dioxide released by human activity, decreasing the **pH** value of the oceans' water and moving it from its alkaline state toward a **neutral** one. If this process continues **unabated**, it is calculated that by about the year 2100, it could **disrupt** marine ecosystems, threatening the existence of much marine life and preventing the oceans from carrying out their current environmental functions. 35

NOTES

microorganism 微生物　**invisible** 見えない　**marine algae** 海藻　**fungi** 菌類　**worm** 蠕虫 （ぜんちゅう）　**mollusc** 軟体動物　**sea lion** アシカ　**sea otter** ラッコ　**seal** アザラシ **polar bear** シロクマ　**sea urchin** ウニ　**population** 個体数　**kelp** 昆布　**organism** 生命体 **nitrogen** 窒素　**beset** 悩まされる　**non-biodegradable** 微生物で分解できない　**accumulate** 蓄積する　**food chain** 食物連鎖　**pH** 水素（イオン）指数　**neutral** 中性の　**unabated** 衰えな い　**disrupt** 〜を破壊する

Comprehension Check

Choose the most suitable answer for each question.

1. According to the passage, why is the ocean considered an "unknown kingdom"?
   (a) Although scientists know them well, regular people rarely get the opportunity to become familiar with them.
   (b) In a survey, most people were able to name only the Pacific and Atlantic oceans.
   (c) Most of the land area covered by the oceans is unexplored.

2. Which of the following statements is NOT true of microorganisms.
   (a) We can see them everywhere.
   (b) They are important in marine ecosystems.
   (c) They account for more than half of the living things in the oceans.

3. Why are marine mammals under particular threat?
   (a) They are especially sensitive to plastic.
   (b) They cannot distinguish between biodegradable and non-biodegradable material.
   (c) They generally live in areas impacted heavily by humans.

4. Why is an increased volume of carbon dioxide a problem for the oceans?
   (a) It makes the water less alkaline.
   (b) The oceans expel carbon dioxide, making the atmosphere worse.
   (c) The gas is poisonous to marine animals.

Best Summary

From these four sentences, choose the one that summarizes the passage best.

1. Whales and microbes play the most important roles in marine ecosystems.

2. Too much is unknown about the oceans for scientists to be able to ascertain the health of marine ecosystems.

3. Trash is the main threat to the health of the oceans, and it is important that we stop dumping things there.

4. The oceans hold diverse life and perform important environmental functions, which are now under threat.

Word Choice

Choose a suitable expression to fill each blank.

1. Polar bears keep the Arctic seal population _____.
   (a) on leash   (b) checked out   (c) declined   (d) in check

2. Fishermen _____ healthy seas and oceans for their livelihood.
   (a) depend on   (b) consist of   (c) benefit   (d) reliant

3. Much of the plastic in the ocean consists of small particles _____ in water.
   (a) expended   (b) levitated   (c) suspended   (d) extended

4. More carbon dioxide in the atmosphere leads to _____ in the ocean's pH value.
   (a) an increase   (b) a solution   (c) a decrease   (d) an extension

5. Overfishing can _____ marine ecosystems.
   (a) exacerbate   (b) disrupt   (c) deter   (d) defer

Composition

Rearrange the words within the parentheses to make sentences.

1. 海洋の微生物で分解できないプラスチックゴミは環境問題専門家たちを大いに心配させる問題である。

   Non-biodegradable plastic trash in (an / concerns / environmentalists / is / issue / ocean / that / the) greatly.

2. 私たちはプラスチックゴミを処分するために緊急に何かをすべきであると言う科学者もいる。

Some scientists say that we should (do / get / of / rid / something / to / urgently) plastic trash.

_____

3. ラッコの存在はたくさんのウニが生態系の崩壊を引き起こすことを妨げている。

The presence of sea otters (abundance / an / causing / from / of / prevents / sea / urchins) ecosystem collapse.

_____

4. 海洋哺乳類はどこに生息しているのかということで生息地の喪失の危険にとりわけ晒されている。

Marine mammals are (because / habitat / loss / of / of / particular / threat / under) where they live.

_____

Partial Dictation and Conversation   🎧 1-33

Listen to the dialogue, and fill in the missing words. Then, speak the dialogue with a partner. After speaking once or twice, switch roles.

A: Do you like swimming?

B: Yes, I like it a lot. [1] _____, I often go to the beach in summer.

A: Oh, really? I never knew. That must be a lot of fun.

B: It is, but [2] _____ has been worrying me lately. There is a lot of trash, especially plastic waste. I also heard that there are some dioxins and heavy metals [3] _____ in some places in the sea off Japan.

A: Well, I've heard that the oceans as a whole are in a very serious state. Apparently, there's pollution nearly everywhere, and the oceans [4] _____ acidification.

B: That sounds terrible. [5] _____ there's anything we should be doing to address the problem.

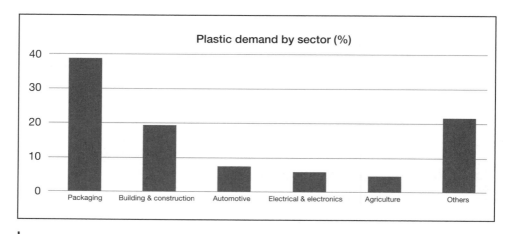

Active Learning

As described in the passage, plastic trash is a major problem in the oceans. The chart below shows how much plastic different economic sectors use. With a partner, talk about the information in the chart, including the questions below.

1. Which economic sectors use the most plastic?

2. Which sectors use the least plastic?

3. Thinking about your daily life, can you think of any ways the plastic trash situation might be improved?

[Data source: http://www.gesamp.org/publications/microplastics-in-the-marine-environment-part-2]

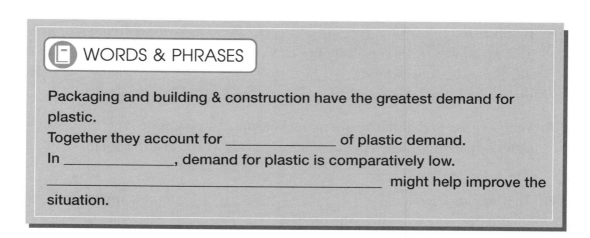

WORDS & PHRASES

Packaging and building & construction have the greatest demand for plastic.

Together they account for _____ of plastic demand.

In _____, demand for plastic is comparatively low.

_____ might help improve the situation.

UNIT 6

Powering Our World

クリーンエネルギー

化石燃料から再生可能エネルギーへの移行が世界各国で進められている。それぞれの国の自然環境から得られる地熱、ダム、風力、太陽光、波力、バイオマスなどがどのようにクリーンエネルギーを生んでいるのかを読み解こう。

Vocabulary Preview

Match each word with a definition by drawing a line between them.

1. decade

2. exhaustion

3. fossil

4. disruption

5. fluctuation

6. climate

7. volcano

8. biofuel

9. controversial

10. investment

(a) a break or interruption in something

(b) a fuel made from plant or animal sources

(c) a mountain with a hole at the top through which hot gases and lava escape

(d) causing a lot of disagreement

(e) a change in a level or amount

(f) a situation where the supply of something has been used up

(g) a period of 10 years

(h) an animal or plant that lived long ago and has been preserved

(i) putting money or time into something in the hope of future gain

(j) typical weather conditions

Ever since the last decades of the 19th century, people have been expressing concern regarding the exhaustion of fossil fuel resources and the need to move to **renewable** sources of energy. It took about a century for action to be taken, with wind turbines appearing in the 1970s, followed by **solar farms** in the 1980s. Since then,

5 technological progress has made these and other renewable energy technologies more efficient; at the same time, disruptions in the supply and fluctuations in the price of fossil fuels, along with fears of pollution and climate change, have served as incentives to **accelerate** the switch. A number of countries are leading the way.

Iceland generates almost 100 percent of its electricity from renewable sources,

10 most of it **geothermal** power. That is impressive, but it is important to bear in mind that Iceland has a unique landscape with hundreds of volcanoes and hot springs. That means that it cannot really serve as a model for the rest of the world. Another country getting nearly all of its electricity from renewable sources is Costa Rica. In this case, the majority of the country's electricity needs is generated by **hydroelectric**

15 plants. This is made possible by its large number of rivers and high rainfall. It also has a small population, making it possible to build large numbers of dams to generate the electricity it needs. Again, the lessons for other countries are limited.

Sweden aims to reach 100 percent renewable electricity production by 2040. The country generates wind power, solar power, and wave power, and also makes

20 biofuels. A significant proportion of the electricity generated in Sweden, as in Costa Rica, comes from hydroelectric plants. The country also has three large nuclear power plants, which generate around one-third of the country's electricity needs. Safety concerns of course make this dependence highly controversial, and Sweden is moving to **decommission** the nuclear power plants gradually over the coming

25 decades. It will be interesting to see how the country fills in the gaps.

Uruguay generates about 95 percent of its electricity from renewable sources. Some of that is accounted for by hydroelectric plants, but in recent years Uruguay has not built any more hydroelectric **capacity**, instead focusing on wind power, **biomass**, and solar power. The country does not have any nuclear plants. The country's success

30 with renewable energy appears to stem mainly from government policies that create a favorable climate for investment in renewable energy generation. For example,

businesses building **wind farms** are offered a **guaranteed** price for the electricity generated for 20 years after construction, meaning that, even with **unforeseeable** market changes, they can still make a profit.

Learning from examples such as those covered here, it is to be hoped that more 35 and more countries will accelerate the move to renewable energy sources.

NOTES

renewable 再生可能な　**solar farm** 太陽光発電所　**accelerate** ～を加速する　**geothermal** 地熱の　**hydroelectric** 水力発電の　**decommission** ～を閉鎖する　**capacity** 能力
biomass バイオマス（代替エネルギーの供給源としての植物）　**wind farm** 風力発電所
guaranteed 保証された　**unforeseeable** 予測不可能な

Comprehension Check

Choose the most suitable answer for each question.

1. Which factor is NOT mentioned as contributing to accelerated development in renewable energy since the late 20th century?
   (a) fossil fuel price changes
   (b) fears of climate change
   (c) government subsidies

2. Why is Costa Rica not the best renewable energy generation model for the rest of the world?
   (a) It has hundreds of volcanoes.
   (b) It has a small population and many rivers.
   (c) It does not have the engineering capabilities to build enough dams.

3. What is controversial about Sweden's electricity policies?
   (a) A large proportion of the country's power is generated by nuclear power.
   (b) Its 100 percent renewable electricity production target is very ambitious.
   (c) It is very similar to Costa Rica.

4. What is the main lesson to be learned from Uruguay?
   (a) The country does not use hydroelectric power.
   (b) The country has a good balance between green energy and nuclear power.
   (c) Government policies make investment in renewable energy attractive.

Best Summary

From these four sentences, choose the one that summarizes the passage best.

1. Imitating Iceland or Costa Rica is the best way for most countries to move toward 100 percent renewable energy.

2. For most countries, it is best to have a mixture of power generation methods including nuclear power, oil, and coal.

3. It is important to move to more renewable energy by studying success stories in a variety of countries.

4. The experience of many countries is that the only way to encourage renewable energy generation is to guarantee electricity prices for about 20 years.

Word Choice

Choose a suitable expression to fill each blank.

1. A very large _____ of the electricity generated in Uruguay comes from renewable sources.
   (a) ration   (b) rationale   (c) portion   (d) proportion

2. In Japan, solar power is estimated to _____ 6.8 percent of total electricity generation.
   (a) count for   (b) account for   (c) count on   (d) accede to

3. It may be advisable to avoid too much _____ on nuclear power.
   (a) totality   (b) dependent   (c) reliant   (d) dependence

4. It is _____ when 100 percent renewable electricity will be realized.
   (a) unforeseeable   (b) impredictable   (c) foresight   (d) delightful

5. Recent increases in solar power generation are _____ attributable to technological advances.
   (a) principled   (b) main   (c) mainly   (d) principal

Composition

Rearrange the words within the parentheses to make sentences.

1. 多くの場合、環境に優しい発電への移行を成功させるには、堅実な政府の政策が必要である。

   In most cases, success in transitioning (electricity / environmentally / from / generation / sound / stems / to) sound government policies.

2. ドイツは2038年までに石炭を使うのを完全にやめることを目標に設定している。
   Germany (aims / by / coal / entirely / stop / to / using) the year 2038.

   _____

3. 厳しい環境規制を導入することの大きな課題は、企業が利益を得る方法がなければならないことである。
   A big challenge to introducing strict environmental regulations is that there has (a / be / companies / for / make / to / to / way) a profit.

   _____

4. ひとつの国が従来続けられているものからグリーン電力の発電に移行するには一般的には何年もかかる。
   (a / country / for / generally / it / many / takes / years) to transition from conventional to green electricity generation.

   _____

Partial Dictation and Conversation

Listen to the dialogue, and fill in the missing words. Then, speak the dialogue with a partner. After speaking once or twice, switch roles.

A: Hi, what have you been up to? I haven't seen you ①_____.

B: Oh, hi, I've been abroad ②_____. I went to the U.S., Canada, Finland, and the Netherlands.

A: Wow, I can understand going to the U.S. and Canada in one trip. But Europe is so far ③_____ and from the U.S.

B: Yes, I know. But my main purpose was to see some interesting power stations. I went to Alholmens Kraft in Finland, Annapolis Tidal Station in Canada, and the Hoover Dam in the U.S.

A: ④_____ the Hoover Dam, and I understand that Annapolis generates tidal power. What about Alholmens Kraft?

B: That one ⑤_____ biofuel, mainly bark and wood chips from the timber industry based on the nearby forests.

Active Learning ➤

The table below shows the approximate percentage of electricity production accounted for in four countries by natural gas, coal, nuclear power, and renewable energy sources. Talk about the data with a partner, including the questions below.

1. Which of the four energy sources accounts for the highest percentage of power generation in each country?

2. Which of the four energy sources accounts for the lowest percentage of power generation in each country?

3. Do you find anything surprising about the data?

Percentage of electricity production accounted for by four sources in four countries, 2012-2019

DESCRIPTION	U.S.	FRANCE	INDIA	UK
Natural gas	29.0	3.6	6.9	42.0
Coal	14.0	4.1	56.1	9.0
Nuclear	9.0	76.6	1.9	21.0
Renewables	11.0	17.8	30.1	24.5

[Data sources: https://en.wikipedia.org/wiki/Energy_in_the_United_States
https://www.energy-uk.org.uk/our-work/generation/electricity-generation.html
https://en.wikipedia.org/wiki/Electricity_sector_in_France#Fossil_Fuels
https://en.wikipedia.org/wiki/Electricity_sector_in_India]

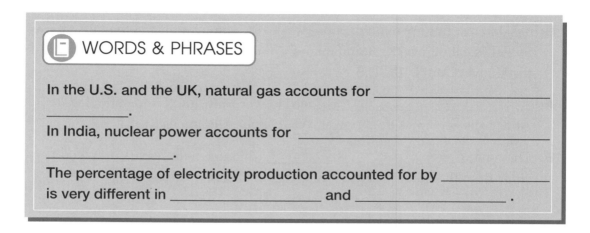

WORDS & PHRASES

In the U.S. and the UK, natural gas accounts for _____
_____.

In India, nuclear power accounts for _____
_____.

The percentage of electricity production accounted for by _____
is very different in _____ and _____ .

UNIT 7

Hot, Powerful, and Clean

太陽光発電

再生可能エネルギー源として太陽光に対する注目が増している。太陽光はどこでも手に入るものなので、様々な面で多くの利点があり、太陽光発電の技術開発も進んでいるが、今後の技術開発も興味深い。

Vocabulary Preview

Match each word with a definition by drawing a line between them.

1. rapid •   • (a) an important new discovery or advance

2. annual •   • (b) to control; to have the largest share of something

3. crucial •   • (c) a short electromagnetic wave

4. gravity •   • (d) in one year

5. breakthrough •   • (e) fast

6. dominate •   • (f) likely to be successful

7. significant •   • (g) a force that pulls things towards an object

8. constant •   • (h) extremely important

9. microwave •   • (i) happening all the time

10. viable •   • (j) meaningful

Solar power is perhaps the best-known renewable energy source. It is currently undergoing rapid development in an attempt to reduce our dependence on fossil fuels, which are quickly being **depleted** and have been identified as the main cause of climate change. Currently, solar power generates only about 1.3 percent of the world's electricity. In addition, as far as **mainstream** renewable energy sources are concerned, it comes third in terms of annual generation capacity behind hydropower and wind power. However, the **International Energy Agency** (IEA) believes that solar power has by far the greatest **potential** of all energy sources. Worldwide generation capacity is growing at a rate of about 35 percent a year, and the IEA
10 forecasts that solar power may provide more than a quarter of the world's electricity by the middle of the century.

In addition to the fact that solar power is renewable — indeed, **inexhaustible** — a key advantage of solar power is that, once the generating capacity is built, there is no need for ongoing imports. This enhances countries' energy security, a crucial
15 consideration when you consider the costs to the economy of a sharp rise in fossil fuel prices and the danger that **political tensions** between nations could disrupt supplies.

Until recently, most work in solar power was based in Europe, and Spain, for example, has some of the largest solar power stations in the world. But now the center of gravity has moved to Asia, particularly Japan and China. Japan is one of the
20 world's solar technology leaders; one recent breakthrough there is a new type of thin and cheap **solar cell** that can be attached to walls and even curved surfaces, making it possible to generate power in places where that has **hitherto** been impossible. However, production costs in Japan are high, and government policy does not seem to be **well-tailored** to the needs of companies. As a result, expansion of the domestic
25 market has stalled, and China has come to dominate the world market.

Solar technologies can be divided into two broad categories: **passive solar** and **active solar**. Passive **measures** — such as choice of building materials and **orienting** buildings so that they face the sun — can make a significant difference. The range of active solar technologies is now very large, and constant technological
30 **innovation** serves to increase generation capacity and lower costs. One of the most effective technologies currently is **concentrated solar power**, which uses lenses and

mirrors to concentrate the sun's rays into a focused beam. Another technology that is being explored is space-based solar power, in which the power generated would be **transmitted** to the Earth via microwave. Although it still requires technological advances to become feasible and is far from becoming commercially viable, the amount of energy that can be collected in space is so much greater than on the Earth that it holds great interest for scientists and policymakers. 35

NOTES

deplete 〜を激減させる　**mainstream** 主流の
International Energy Agency 国際エネルギー機関　**potential** 可能性
inexhaustible 無尽蔵な　**political tension** 政治的緊張　**solar cell** 太陽電池
hitherto これまで　**well-tailored** しっかり調整された　**passive solar** 受動的な太陽光
（太陽光発電などの設備に頼らず、太陽光や風などの自然エネルギーを利用したもの）
active solar 能動的な太陽光（太陽光発電などの施設によって自然エネルギーを利用したもの）
measure 手段　**orient** 〜の向きを（適切に）調整する　**innovation** 革新　**concentrated**
solar power 集光型太陽熱発電　**transmit** 〜を送る

Comprehension Check

Choose the most suitable answer for each question.

1. Which of the following is NOT true of solar power?
   (a) It generates less power than hydropower does.
   (b) Generation capacity is growing rapidly.
   (c) Currently, it generates about 13 percent of the world's electricity.

2. Why is solar power good from the viewpoint of energy security?
   (a) It does not need ongoing imports.
   (b) Solar power stations are easy to defend from attack.
   (c) It is easy to get support from Europe.

3. What is NOT true about Japan?
   (a) The domestic market is expanding rapidly.
   (b) It has developed thin solar cells that can be attached to curved surfaces.
   (c) There appear to be some problems with government policies.

4. How does concentrated solar power work?
   (a) It generates power in space.
   (b) It makes solar power into a focused beam using lenses and mirrors.
   (c) It is a passive technology.

Best Summary

From these four sentences, choose the one that summarizes the passage best.

1. Of renewable energy sources, solar power is currently third but is growing rapidly thanks to a range of new technologies.

2. For alternative energy investors, Asia is now the best market, followed by Europe and the U.S.

3. Until now, the focus in solar energy has been on active technologies, but experts suggest a shift in focus to passive technologies.

4. Once a few remaining technological problems are solved and space-based solar power becomes cheaper, it will provide for all our energy needs.

Word Choice

Choose a suitable expression to fill each blank.

1. New solar power technologies _____ scientists.
   (a) has considerable interest for   (b) largely interesting
   (c) hold great interest for   (d) have big concern for

2. There is a scenario _____ the world is still almost totally dependent on fossil fuels in 2050.
   (a) whereof   (b) therefore   (c) in which   (d) henceforth

3. This, our seventh solar power station, represents our _____ commitment to renewable energy.
   (a) interrupted   (b) ongoing   (c) continually   (d) continue

4. Wind power, tidal power, and solar power have the advantage of being practically _____.
   (a) inexhaustible   (b) unfatigued   (c) tireless   (d) exhausted

5. _____ commercial viability, space-based solar power has a long way to go.
   (a) When consider   (b) In principle   (c) In fact   (d) In terms of

Composition

Rearrange the words within the parentheses to make sentences.

1. 太陽光発電は全体として再生可能エネルギーよりも少なくとも2倍高い割合で増加しているということを研究者たちは発見した。

Researchers have found that solar power is growing (a / at / at / higher / least / rate / times / two) than renewable energy as a whole.

_____

2. 太陽光発電から得られる可能性のあるエネルギー量は、他のエネルギー源から得られるものよりもはるかに多い。

The amount of energy that could be harvested from solar power is (from / greater / much / other / so / than / that) energy sources.

_____

3. 発電技術は従来型と代替型という2つのタイプに分類できると言われる。

It is said that electricity (be / can / divided / generation / into / technologies / two / types): conventional and alternative.

_____

4. 太陽熱を単純利用した技術は、ほとんどゼロの投資で相当量の電気を生み出すのを可能にする。

Passive solar (amounts / generate / it / makes / possible / significant / technology / to) of electricity with nearly zero investment.

_____

Partial Dictation and Conversation

🎧 1-44

Listen to the dialogue, and fill in the missing words. Then, speak the dialogue with a partner. After speaking once or twice, switch roles.

A: When we were talking about your trip, you didn't mention
1 _____ in the Netherlands.

B: Oh, yes, I went to see the Energy Observer 2 _____.

A: What's that?

B: It's a boat 3 _____ the sun, hydrogen, and wind. Shipping is a major mode of transportation, so it's important to develop environmentally sound ships.

A: Mmm, I see. So was that 4 _____ a holiday?

B: Well, it was fun, but 5 _____ to get a job in the renewable energy sector, so I also had a practical purpose.

Look at the chart below, which shows the amount of solar photovoltaic generating capacity added over four years in four countries. Talk with a partner about the differences between the four countries and the overall trends. Include the following questions.

1. How do the four countries compare in terms of solar PV generation capacity added?

2. What trends can you see in the data from 2015?

3. What happened in 2018?

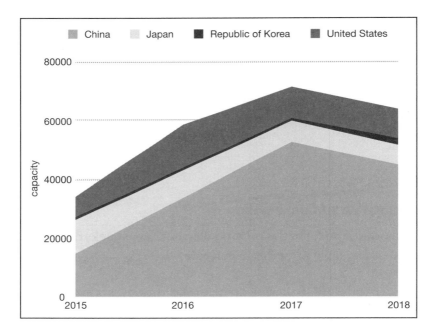

[Data source: https://en.wikipedia.org/wiki/Solar_power_by_country]

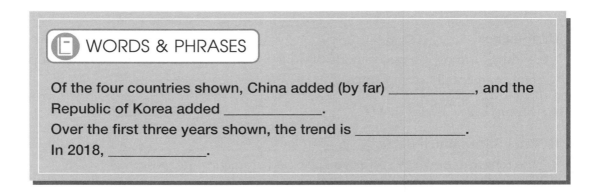

WORDS & PHRASES

Of the four countries shown, China added (by far) _____, and the Republic of Korea added _____.
Over the first three years shown, the trend is _____.
In 2018, _____.

UNIT 8 Keep on Running

水の重要性

水は生命が存続するのに絶対に必要なものである。地球上の大部分を覆っていて、水は循環していると言われるが、そのメカニズムはどうなっているのか。人間は水をどのように利用しているかを知ろう。

Vocabulary Preview

Match each word with a definition by drawing a line between them.

1. essential • • (a) absolutely necessary

2. planet • • (b) a river of ice

3. property • • (c) a large body that moves around a star

4. atmosphere • • (d) can be seen

5. hail • • (e) the air surrounding the planet

6. spring • • (f) frozen raindrops that fall as balls of ice

7. glacier • • (g) to move goods or people

8. visible • • (h) extremely important and necessary

9. transport • • (i) a feature or quality of something

10. vital • • (j) a place where water comes naturally up from underground

That water is essential to our lives is well-known. Water covers more than 70 percent of the surface of our planet. It also accounts for about 70 percent of humans' body weight. It is a fascinating substance with a **deceptively** simple chemical structure of two **hydrogen atoms** bonded to a single **oxygen** atom. It is the only
5 common substance that exists as a **solid**, a **liquid**, and a gas on the Earth's surface. It is unusual in that it is less **dense** in solid form than as a liquid. This property means that ice forms at the top of a lake in winter, **insulating** the water below from getting too cold and allowing fishes and other life to survive the winter.

Water moves around the planet in what is known as the **hydrologic cycle**. It
10 **evaporates** from the seas and oceans into the atmosphere, from where much of it falls back into the oceans as rain. Some of it is carried **inland** by winds, where it falls onto the land, usually as rain but sometimes as snow or hail. Some of that water will fall into rivers, from where its passage back to the seas and oceans is quite direct. Much of the water will fall onto the land. From there, it may flow over the ground
15 and find its way to a river; or it may **seep** into the soil, helping to grow plants. Once underground, the water may feed freshwater springs or lakes, or flow towards rivers or oceans.

The system involving all the water found on the Earth and in its atmosphere is **collectively** known as the **hydrosphere**. It is calculated that as much as 97.5 percent
20 of the hydrosphere consists of salt water, which is difficult for humans to make direct use of. Humans are more concerned with fresh water. Of the total amount of fresh water on the planet, a large majority is **trapped** in glaciers, although climate change is resulting in accelerated release of that water. About a third is groundwater, and less than one percent is found in rivers and lakes.

25 Humans, of course, use fresh water daily for drinking and for bathing. We also use it for cooking and washing things. Beyond these most visible uses, water plays a major role in the world economy. About 70 percent of the fresh water we use goes to agriculture. More obviously, fishing of course depends on water. Many of the things we buy from day to day have been transported across the oceans on ships.

30 Because water is so vital to our lives, it is important to look after it. Shortages of water, **desertification**, flooding, water pollution — all these problems and more

demand **imaginative** solutions.

NOTES

deceptively 見かけによらず　**hydrogen** 水素　**atom** 原子　**oxygen** 酸素　**solid** 固体
liquid 液体　**dense** 高密度の　**insulate** 〜を覆う　**hydrologic cycle** 水循環（太陽エネル
ギーを主因として引き起こされる地球における継続的な水の循環のこと。）　**evaporate** 蒸発する
inland 内陸に　**seep** 浸透する　**collectively** まとめて　**hydrosphere** 水圏（地球の表面の水
の占める部分）　**trap** 〜を閉じ込める　**desertification** 砂漠化　**imaginative** 独創的な

Comprehension Check

Choose the most suitable answer for each question.

1. Which of the following is NOT true of water?
    (a) It consists of two oxygen atoms and one hydrogen atom.
    (b) It exists in gas, liquid, and solid forms on the surface of the Earth.
    (c) It is denser as a liquid than as a solid.

2. What is the hydrologic cycle?
    (a) It is the flow of water in the oceans.
    (b) It is the way hydrogen circulates through the atmosphere.
    (c) It is the way water moves around the planet.

3. What can be said about fresh water?
    (a) Probably only about 2.5 percent of the water on the planet is fresh water.
    (b) Most of the Earth's fresh water is in rivers and lakes.
    (c) It accounts for most of the water on the planet.

4. Which is NOT true about the uses of fresh water?
    (a) It is important in the world economy.
    (b) Most of it is used for drinking.
    (c) Most of it is used in agriculture.

Best Summary

From these four sentences, choose the one that summarizes the passage best.

1. The world has too much salt water, and it is necessary for us to implement desalination in order to reduce it.

2. Water is ubiquitous on our planet and essential to our lives.

3. It is important that we reduce drastically the amount of water that we use in our daily lives.

4. In order to improve understanding of the hydrosphere, it is important to increase our efforts in education.

Word Choice

Choose a suitable expression to fill each blank.

1. Increased use of water for intensive agriculture is leading to _____ depletion of underground water resources.
   (a) velocity   (b) accelerated   (c) vapid   (d) speed

2. As water becomes more scarce, farmers may have to move away from agricultural activities _____ excessive use of water, such as raising cattle.
   (a) involving   (b) required   (c) do   (d) acquiring

3. In hot weather, rainfall tends to _____ extremely quickly.
   (a) radiate   (b) condense   (c) transpire   (d) evaporate

4. Most substances are _____ as solids than as liquids.
   (a) densest   (b) sparser   (c) denser   (d) less dense

5. Ice at the top of a lake plays a vital _____ in keeping the lake habitable in winter.
   (a) roll   (b) rule   (c) role   (d) stage

Composition

Rearrange the words within the parentheses to make sentences.

1. 豊富な水に慣れた人たちが節約できるようになるのは難しい。
   (accustomed / difficult / for / is / it / people / to) plentiful water to learn to economize.

2. 水資源を浪費しないことに成功することは、すべての人の懸命な努力にかかっている。

   Our success in conserving water resources (best / depends / doing / everyone / on / their / very).

   _____

3. 地球の気象のほとんどは、惑星の表面に最も近い大気圏の一部である、対流圏として知られるところで起こる。

   Most of the Earth's weather (as / in / is / known / occurs / the / troposphere / what), the part of the atmosphere nearest to the planet's surface.

   _____

4. 文明が繁栄するようにするのはとりわけ真水の供給である。

   It is above (all / allow / civilizations / fresh water / of / supplies / that) to flourish.

   _____

Partial Dictation and Conversation　　🎧 1-50

Listen to the dialogue, and fill in the missing words. Then, speak the dialogue with a partner. After speaking once or twice, switch roles.

A: How much water [1] _____ you use every day?

B: Mmm, that's a difficult question. I've [2] _____ about it.

A: Well, [3] _____, everyone drinks some water or other drinks containing water.

B: That's true. And I guess everyone uses some water for cooking and so on.

A: Yes. And then [4] _____ having a bath and flushing the toilet.

B: Oh, yes, I hadn't thought of that. I guess we all use [5] _____ amount.

Active Learning

Look at the charts below, which show the typical daily water needs of four kinds of animal, followed by a categorization of how humans typically use water. Talk about the charts with a partner, including the questions below.

1. Which of the animals shown uses the most water?

2. Of non-human animals, which uses the most water and which uses the least?

3. What can you say about human uses of water?

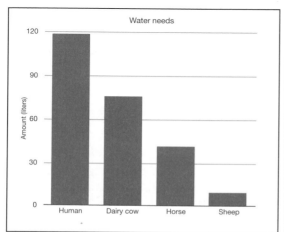
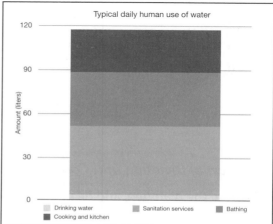

[Data source: https://en.wikipedia.org/wiki/Fresh_water]

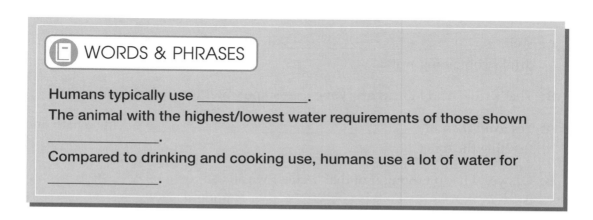

WORDS & PHRASES

Humans typically use _____.

The animal with the highest/lowest water requirements of those shown

_____.

Compared to drinking and cooking use, humans use a lot of water for

_____.

UNIT 9

Where Are All the Trees?

深刻な森林破壊の現状

かつての地球は森林が生い茂っていた。人間が始めた農業や経済的利益のために、木々が切り倒されている。その結果として、地球の温暖化につながったり、熱帯雨林の多くの種が絶滅の危機に瀕している。

Vocabulary Preview

Match each word with a definition by drawing a line between them.

1. agriculture
2. quantity
3. measure
4. absorb
5. vicious cycle
6. extinction
7. phenomenon
8. function
9. ingredient
10. cattle

(a) cows and bulls kept for milk or meat

(b) to take something in gradually

(c) the disappearance of an animal or plant

(d) a purpose or role

(e) the number or amount of something

(f) something that happens in society or exists naturally

(g) an action taken to deal with a problem

(h) growing crops and raising animals for food

(i) a basic item from which a food is made

(j) a situation in which one problem causes another problem, which contributes to the first problem in turn

When humans invented agriculture some 11,000 years ago, forests covered nearly two-thirds of the Earth's surface. The current figure is around one-third, meaning that humans have cut down about half of the world's total quantity of trees. The pace of **deforestation** has picked up dramatically in recent decades, with an
5 area the size of Washington State, or half the size of Japan, disappearing most years. If **drastic** measures are not taken to slow down the rate at which forests are cleared, all forestland could be gone in a century.

Trees trap carbon. When forested land is cleared, that carbon is released into the atmosphere. As the amount of carbon dioxide in the atmosphere increases, the
10 greenhouse effect is strengthened, thus contributing to global warming. At the same time as the amount of carbon dioxide is increased, the number of trees available to absorb it is decreased, contributing to a vicious cycle, as with so many environmental problems.

Forests, especially tropical rainforests, are the habitat of around 80 percent
15 of the world's species. Naturally, then, loss of forests leads to habitat loss and the extinction of many species. As well as being a sad phenomenon in its own right, these extinctions hold other environmental dangers, as the lost species may have performed important but poorly understood ecological functions.

Most forest clearing happens for agriculture. Planting **palm** trees for palm oil,
20 an ingredient of many **processed** foods and other goods, is one of the most popular uses. **Ranching**, in which cattle are raised in order to produce beef, is another popular use. Deforested land is also sometimes used for **mining**. Another use is **logging**. Logging has a **two-fold** effect on the forest: in addition to the direct loss of trees, a lot of land also has to be cleared for roads to enable the logs to be transported
25 out of the forest. Deforestation also sometimes happens in response to **urban sprawl**: as a city becomes crowded, the crowding is **alleviated** by cutting down the forest around the city, allowing new building to occur.

The people and companies logging or building new farms have the potential to earn a lot of money from their activities and may resist attempts to stop them doing
30 so. This economic aspect of deforestation is what makes it so difficult to stop. Thus, deforestation in Brazil and the **Democratic Republic of the Congo**, for example, is

happening very fast. But in Indonesia, for example, **considerable** reductions have been achieved thanks to strong government-enforced protections for the forests. Let us hope for the spread of such successes.

NOTES

deforestation 森林破壊　**drastic** 思い切った　**palm** ヤシ　**processed** 特別なまたは追加の処理が行われた　**ranching** 大規模放牧　**mining** 採掘　**logging** 伐採　**two-fold** 二重の　**urban sprawl** 都市のスプロール現象（都市が不規則に広がること）　**alleviate** ～を緩和する　**Democratic Republic of the Congo** コンゴ民主共和国　**considerable** かなりの

Comprehension Check

Choose the most suitable answer for each question.

1. How serious is the deforestation problem these days?
   (a) It is no longer as serious as before; scientists think the problem will be solved by the end of the century.
   (b) It is extremely serious: a very large area of forest is lost every year.
   (c) Because deforestation tends to happen in remote areas, no one knows whether it is still happening.

2. What environmental benefits of forests are mentioned?
   (a) They trap carbon and serve agriculture.
   (b) They trap carbon and serve as a habitat for many species.
   (c) They provide logs.

3. Why do people clear forests?
   (a) They clear them for a variety of reasons but mainly for agriculture.
   (b) Mining and logging are the main reasons.
   (c) They do it to avoid urban sprawl.

4. How successful are efforts to reduce deforestation?
   (a) They are successful in some countries but unsuccessful in others.
   (b) They are going very well.
   (c) They are impossible.

From these four sentences, choose the one that summarizes the passage best.

1. Good ideas for slowing and eventually stopping deforestation are spreading out rapidly from Indonesia and a few other Asian countries.

2. We need to take a balanced approach to deforestation.

3. The main cause of deforestation is people eating too much beef; if everyone became vegetarian, we could solve the problem quite quickly.

4. Deforestation, which threatens the environment in many ways, is happening very fast.

Word Choice

Choose a suitable expression to fill each blank.

1. It is necessary to _____ to protect the forests.
   (a) increase logging   (b) tackle quickly
   (c) maintain habitat loss   (d) take drastic measures

2. Deforestation _____ global warming.
   (a) contributes to   (b) benefits   (c) has an effect for   (d) can occur

3. One way _____ deforestation causes harm is by causing extinctions.
   (a) through what   (b) by through   (c) in which   (d) which leads

4. The economic _____ of deforestation makes it a difficult problem to solve.
   (a) faces   (b) aspect   (c) subjects   (d) trait

5. We need to align the economic and _____ costs of cutting trees.
   (a) effort   (b) achieved   (c) covered   (d) environmental

Composition

Rearrange the words within the parentheses to make sentences.

1. 森林破壊の速度を遅くすると絶滅の危機に瀕した種を救うことができるかもしれない。

   Slowing deforestation may (are / enable / save / species / that / threatened / to / us) with extinction.

2. 森林破壊の削減は、いくつかの国々で政府の規制の結果達成されている。

Reductions in deforestation (achieved / been / countries / have / in / some / thanks / to) government regulations.

_____

3. 非常に多くの環境やその他の問題と同様に、森林破壊は長期的な利益よりも短期的な利益を優先するという問題である。

(and / as / environmental / issues / many / other / so / with), deforestation is a question of prioritizing short-term profit over our long-term interests.

_____

4. 森林が姿を消している速度を究明するのは重要である。

It (at / determine / important / is / rate / the / to / which) the forests are disappearing.

_____

Partial Dictation and Conversation 🎧 1-56

Listen to the dialogue, and fill in the missing words. Then, speak the dialogue with a partner. After speaking once or twice, switch roles.

A: Are you an outdoor person?

B: Yes, I often go hiking, and ⬚1 _____ I sometimes go camping.

A: ⬚2 _____ you must often walk through forests, then?

B: Of course. ⬚3 _____ of Japan is covered by forests.

A: ⬚4 _____ really good for the environment.

B: Well, there are some problems. Most of the planted trees are cedar, and there aren't enough people working in forestry. ⬚5 _____ of trees in Japan, we import very large quantities of wood.

Look at the chart showing the percentage of land in various countries that is forested and, working with a partner, talk about what you see, including the following questions.

1. Can you see any general tendency within Asia?

2. Which countries have particularly high proportions of forested land?

3. Which country or countries have particularly low proportions of forested land?

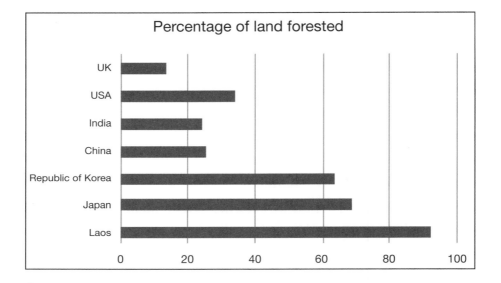

[Data source: https://data.worldbank.org/indicator/ag.lnd.frst.zs]

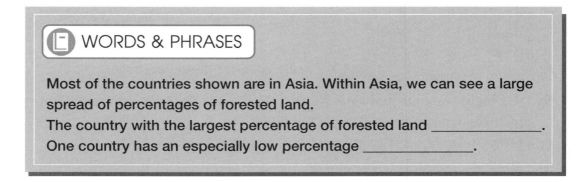

WORDS & PHRASES

Most of the countries shown are in Asia. Within Asia, we can see a large spread of percentages of forested land.
The country with the largest percentage of forested land _____.
One country has an especially low percentage _____.

UNIT 10

Too Hot to Live?

気象変動がもたらすもの

化石燃料の使いすぎによる大気中の二酸化炭素量の増加が地球温暖化の原因であり、地球規模の問題となっている。工業化を遂げた先進国とこれから工業化を目指す開発途上国とのバランスをとることが重要である。

Vocabulary Preview

Match each word with a definition by drawing a line between them.

1. methane •
2. undergo •
3. fluctuate •
4. current •
5. eruption •
6. orbit •
7. consequence •
8. balance •
9. contentious •
10. relinquish •

• (a) an explosion from a volcano
• (b) a gas that is used as a fuel
• (c) to give something up
• (d) to do with the present time
• (e) a curved path around a planet
• (f) causing disagreement
• (g) to consider the importance of two things appropriately
• (h) to move up and down
• (i) the result of an action or process
• (j) to experience something

Scientists have calculated that, since the beginning of the **Industrial Revolution** in the middle of the 18th century, carbon dioxide levels have risen by more than 30 percent and methane levels by a **staggering** 140 percent or more. When considering such figures, it is important to remember that, although two or three centuries seem

5   like a long time to us, the climate typically undergoes large changes over the course of thousands of years. The amount of carbon dioxide in the atmosphere fluctuated between about 180 **parts per million** (ppm) and 300 ppm for a few hundred thousand years until 1950, after which it has continued a rapid rise to its current level of about 405 ppm.

10   The Earth's climate is **regulated** by many different factors, and it is impossible for us to do anything about some important ones, such as volcanic eruptions or **variations** in solar **radiation** or in the Earth's orbit. Those factors that are under the control of humans are called **anthropogenic**. There is still some **disagreement** about the **severity** of climate change, to what degree it is anthropogenic, and how

15   much effort we should make to prevent it or slow it down. However, a large majority of scientists believe that the rapid rise in atmospheric carbon, and the greenhouse effect that it causes, cannot **reasonably** be explained in any other way than as the effect of using too much fossil fuel. This has radically affected the planet's energy budget (the balance of energy coming in and going out), tipping the scale toward

20   more and more **accumulation** of energy and **consequently** rising temperatures.

Predicting the future is naturally more difficult than recreating what happened in the past. We depend on scientific models, which differ somewhat from research group to research group. **Depressingly**, even with radical action, some of the changes already occurring can no longer be stopped and will take many years or decades to

25   play out. But most models agree that the consequences of not taking radical action will be **disastrous**.

What kind of action to take, and how much and how quickly, are **inevitably** political more than scientific decisions. Politicians need to balance long-term dangers against the **urgent** concerns of the day, and the short-term interests of their

30   own citizens against the needs of the planet. One contentious issue is that current global warming can largely be attributed to the industrialization of countries in

Europe and North America, most of which have become wealthy thanks to that industrialization. Reducing greenhouse gas **emissions** will depend to a large extent on less-industrialized and less-wealthy nations, which are reluctant to relinquish the benefits of economic development taken for granted by richer societies. 35

NOTES

Industrial Revolution 産業革命 **staggering** 非常に驚かせるほどの **parts per million** 100万分のいくらであるかを示す単位 **regulate** 〜を制御する **variation** 変化 **radiation** 放射線 **anthropogenic** 人間が原因の **disagreement** 論争 **severity** 重大性 **reasonably** 合理的に **accumulation** 蓄積 **consequently** その結果として **depressingly** 悲しくなるほど **disastrous** 悲惨な **inevitably** 必然的に **urgent** 緊急の **emission** 排出

Comprehension Check

Choose the most suitable answer for each question.

1. Which of the following is true of changes in the atmosphere since the Industrial Revolution?
   (a) The amount of methane has more than doubled.
   (b) The amount of oxygen has decreased.
   (c) The amount of all gases has fluctuated unpredictably.

2. Which of the following is NOT true?
   (a) It is not possible for humans to change some of the things that influence the climate.
   (b) The amount of atmospheric carbon has increased considerably.
   (c) Scientists agree that fossil fuel use is not connected to climate change.

3. What is said about the necessity for action?
   (a) It is unnecessary to do anything special.
   (b) Failing to take action will probably bring disastrous consequences.
   (c) We should wait to take action until all scientists agree on a model.

4. What is true about the contentious issue described in the final paragraph?
   (a) Most less-wealthy nations do not believe that climate change is real.
   (b) Less-wealthy nations would like to enjoy the economic benefits of industrialization.
   (c) New technologies will allow less-wealthy nations to industrialize without environmental cost.

Best Summary

From these four sentences, choose the one that summarizes the passage best.

1. In order to slow down anthropogenic climate change, it is important that radical action be taken.

2. It seems unlikely that humans will be able to do anything to reduce the effects of climate change.

3. Industrialized and developing nations do not agree on climate change.

4. There are major differences between the climate models of leading scientists, leading to great confusion among the general public.

Word Choice

Choose a suitable expression to fill each blank.

1. To solve such a serious problem, modest measures will not be enough; instead, _____ measures are called for.
   (a) radical   (b) considerate   (c) comprehensible   (d) smaller

2. _____ countries have signed up to the Kyoto Protocol on climate change.
   (a) Most of   (b) Almost   (c) A majority of   (d) Mostly

3. Politicians find it difficult to reach agreement over _____ the problem of climate change.
   (a) how serious   (b) how severe   (c) how seriously is   (d) the severity of

4. Adjusting our economies to take the environment into account will _____ involve some difficulties.
   (a) incredibly   (b) presumptively   (c) inevitably   (d) incredible

5. The success in getting most countries to sign up to the Kyoto Protocol can be _____, at least in part, to the dedication of climate scientists.
   (a) attributed   (b) blamed   (c) contributed   (d) thanks

Composition

Rearrange the words within the parentheses to make sentences.

1. 生き方を変える必要性が極めて明らかだとしても、人は一般に生き方を変えたがらない。

   People are generally (change / even / life / of / reluctant / their / to / way) if the necessity is very clear.

2. 先進産業国経済では、私たちの比較的高い生活水準を当たり前だと考えがちである。

In the advanced industrial economies, (easy / for / granted / is / it / take / to) our relatively high standards of living.

_____

3. 現代社会は予測可能な気象条件に大部分を依存している。

Modern societies are (a / climatic conditions / dependent / extent / large / on / predictable / to).

_____

4. 地球の温暖化が、今日の私たちの行動の結果として、どの程度、遅くしたり止められるのか完全にはっきりしているわけではない。

It is not (can / clear / completely / degree / global / to / warming / what) be slowed or stopped as a result of our actions today.

_____

Partial Dictation and Conversation

Listen to the dialogue, and fill in the missing words. Then, speak the dialogue with a partner. After speaking once or twice, switch roles.

A: What's your favorite season?

B: ☐1 _____ I like spring best. The flowers come out and the weather is pretty good.

A: ☐2 _____ a bit hot in late spring?

B: Well, it can be a bit uncomfortable sometimes in May when ☐3 _____ and there's no air-conditioning, but overall I like it. I really don't like summer, though.

A: ☐4 _____. In Honshu, occasionally the temperature gets up around 40 degrees.

B: ☐5 _____ compared to the Middle East, though. I read that one city in Kuwait experienced a temperature of 54 degrees back in 2016!

Active Learning

Look at the chart below, which shows changes in average global temperatures from 1880, relative to the period 1951-1980. Discuss the data with a partner, including the questions below.

1. What overall trend can you see?

2. What can you say about the temperature since around the 1970s?

3. How important do you think it is for individuals to do something about climate change?

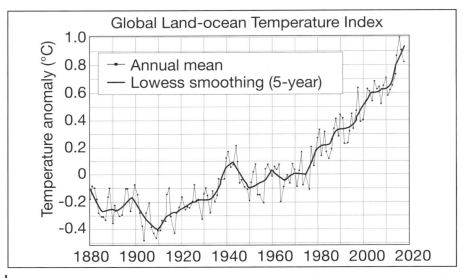

[Data source: By NASA Goddard Institute for Space Studies - http://data.giss.nasa.gov/gistemp/graphs/, Public Domain, https://commons.wikimedia.org/w/index.php?curid=24363898]

WORDS & PHRASES

The graph shows _____.

From about the 1970s, _____.

I (don't) think it is important to _____.

UNIT 11 Reading Anywhere

電子書籍

電子書籍は、専用のリーダーや汎用のタブレット端末や携帯電話にインストールされたアプリで読むことができ、紙の本よりも多くの機能を持っている。紙の書籍に慣れ親しんできた読者はどうするのだろうか。

Vocabulary Preview

Match each word with a definition by drawing a line between them.

1. launch
2. distribution
3. physical
4. specific
5. insert
6. capacity
7. resistance
8. chiefly
9. render
10. profitability

(a) the amount that can be produced or contained

(b) particular

(c) to start something

(d) sharing things among a large number of people in a planned way

(e) connected with the body or an actual thing rather than the mind

(f) the ability to make more money than you put into a business

(g) mostly but not completely

(h) a feeling or force that acts to stop or slow down a change

(i) to put something inside something else

(j) to express or show

Although early e-book projects were launched in the 1960s, it was not until the late 1990s that the technologies necessary for mass distribution came into being, and e-book readers went on general sale. It was in the second half of the first decade of this century that companies like Sony and Amazon released their popular readers

5   that launched the e-book revolution, leading to a situation where, in some countries, sales of e-books are now greater than those of physical books.

A modern e-book reader, or e-book software installed on a **general-purpose** tablet or mobile phone, can hold thousands of books, sorting them by author, title, or date obtained. Usually, it is possible to search inside books or even across books

10   for specific phrases. The software will keep track of where you last read, so it is easy to continue reading where you left off without remembering to insert a bookmark.

Being able to keep all one's books on one small device means there is **theoretically** no longer a need for **crammed** bookshelves in homes, and libraries running out of capacity can stop buying physical books.

15   There are also cost advantages. A **proportion** of the cost of a typical physical book is accounted for by printing, transport, and storage costs. Thus, there is the potential for lower average prices, and indeed major sellers like Amazon often charge less for e-books than for physical books.

Why, then, haven't e-books replaced physical books? Partly, it is surely a

20   question of time. E-book technologies are still young, and the services based on them are introduced at different speeds around the world. Countries also differ in the speed at which they adopt new technologies. As e-books come to be seen as normal, resistance to them is likely to lessen.

There are also a number of issues surrounding e-books that may take a long

25   time to resolve. One e-book seller has reported that customers actually read less than half of their **purchases**. Without the reminder of a cover on a shelf, a reader may never return to a book to finish it. Some other issues chiefly concern academic and other specialist literature. For example, complex layouts and graphics may not be rendered accurately with current technologies. Some publishers are reluctant to

30   sell their e-books to libraries, believing that doing so reduces the potential for sales and thus threatens profitability.

It is often remarked that new technologies tend not to completely replace older technologies. More than a century after the invention of the automobile, there are still people who ride on horseback. In a few decades' time, it will be interesting to see whether owning physical books has become a **niche** practice like using horses for transportation, or if the attractions of physical books mean that they still exist as a major industry.

35

NOTES

general-purpose 汎用の **theoretically** 理論的に **crammed** ぎっしり詰められた
proportion 割合 **purchase** 購入 **niche** 隙間市場

Comprehension Check

Choose the most suitable answer for each question.

1. Which of the following is true regarding the history of e-books?
   (a) E-book readers first went on general sale in the 1960s.
   (b) The idea of e-books came into existence in the 1990s.
   (c) Sony and Amazon released popular e-books this century.

2. Which of the following is NOT mentioned as an advantage of e-books?
   (a) E-books take up less space than physical books.
   (b) E-books have many advanced features for academics.
   (c) It is possible to search inside e-books.

3. What is mentioned as a possible problem with e-books?
   (a) The lack of a physical object reduces their "pull."
   (b) Readers have to pay twice to read the second half of a book.
   (c) Current technology means they cannot be read in a library.

4. What does the passage suggest about the future of e-books?
   (a) They will probably soon replace physical books completely.
   (b) They will probably continue to co-exist with physical books for some time.
   (c) Their limitations mean they are likely to disappear soon.

Best Summary

From these four sentences, choose the one that summarizes the passage best.

1. Due to the many advantages of e-books, it is possible that physical books will die out in the next few years.

2. E-books are superficially convenient but have too many disadvantages to survive in the long term.

3. E-books have gained in popularity rapidly in recent years and may one day replace most physical books.

4. Physical books will disappear at the same time that horses do.

Word Choice

Choose a suitable expression to fill each blank.

1. Resistance to e-books is likely to _____ over time.
(a) deduct (b) lessen (c) reduce (d) minor

2. Many avid readers have books _____ into every available space in their homes.
(a) crammed (b) crumbled (c) packing (d) jumble

3. I _____ read fiction as e-books. I like the feel of a book in my hand.
(a) don't want (b) don't tend (c) tend not to (d) intending to

4. Older people may be slow _____ new technologies.
(a) to adapt (b) to adopt (c) to adapting (d) to adopt for

5. It will be interesting to see the situation with e-books in 20 _____.
(a) year-time (b) years time (c) future years (d) years' time

Composition

Rearrange the words within the parentheses to make sentences.

1. 価格だけに基づいた電子書籍の宣伝は成功しないであろう。つまり、電子書籍には役に立つ機能があるということが重要である。

Advertising of e-books (based / be / is / on / price / solely / to / unlikely) successful; it is important that e-books have useful functions.

2. 国際 ISBN (International Standard Book Number 国際標準図書番号) 機関は、10 桁のコードを使い果たすという懸念のため、2007 年に 13 桁のコードに切り替えた。
The International ISBN Agency switched to 13-digit codes in 2007 because (fears / it / of / of / out / run / that / would) 10-digit codes.

_____

3. 読みの記録をつける電子書籍のソフトウェアの能力は主要な機能である。
The ability (e-book / keep / of / of / software / to / track) your reading is a key function.

_____

4. 紙の書籍では、どこで読むのをやめたのかを記憶しておくことが難しい。
With a physical book, it is (difficult / left / off / remember / to / where / you).

_____

Partial Dictation and Conversation

CD 2-08

Listen to the dialogue, and fill in the missing words. Then, speak the dialogue with a partner. After speaking once or twice, switch roles.

A: Do you do much reading?

B: Well, I am a student! So [1] _____ a lot of reading.

A: Do you do lots of leisure reading, [2] _____ reading for your studies?

B: Well, I do like reading novels, but I have [3] _____ nowadays, so I read less fiction [4] _____. I guess it's only about half an hour a day now.

A: Do you read mainly print books?

B: Most of the books that I need for my studies [5] _____ e-books, so I read them on paper. But I have an e-reader for fiction.

Active Learning

Look at the chart below, with results from surveys conducted by the *Pew Research Center* until 2016 on reading habits of people in the U.S. Discuss the findings with a partner, including the questions below.

1. What proportion of people in the U.S. said in 2016 they had read any book over the previous 12 months?

2. How do the types of book (or book media) compare in terms of popularity?

3. Were there any changes from 2011 to 2016?

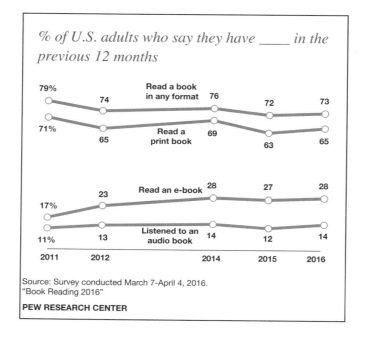

[Data source: "Book Reading 2016." Pew Research Center, Washington, D.C. (September 1, 2016) https:// wvls.org/book-reading-2016-pew-research-study/]

WORDS & PHRASES

Around three-quarters of Americans _____.
Of printed books, e-books, and audiobooks, it appears that _____.
From 2011 to 2016, there was a slight decline _____ and a slight increase in _____.

UNIT 12

Controlling Everything

モノのインターネット

あらゆる情報がネットワーク経由でやりとりできるようになると、私たちの日常生活が劇的に変化するのは確実だ。しかし、ネットワークの監視を怠れば情報が盗み取られる恐れもある。

Vocabulary Preview

Match each word with a definition by drawing a line between them.

1. sensor •
2. principle •
3. transmit •
4. refrigerator •
5. signal •
6. miniaturization •
7. criminal •
8. ubiquitous •
9. surveillance •
10. humidity •

• (a) a machine that keeps things, usually foods, cold

• (b) a basic idea that controls how something works

• (c) someone who does things that are illegal

• (d) a device that reacts to changes in light, pressure, heat, and so on

• (e) the process of observing someone over a long period of time

• (f) can be found everywhere

• (g) a measure of the amount of water in the air

• (h) a sound, light, or electrical message that provides information or an instruction

• (i) the process or technology of making things smaller

• (j) to send information or instructions

A key episode in the development of what is now known as the Internet of Things (IoT) took place in the early 1980s in Pittsburgh's Carnegie Mellon University. It was the **installation** of a drink vending machine equipped with sensors that could be accessed remotely. **Savvy** programmers could check the temperature inside the machine and whether it was stocked, before deciding whether to make the trip to the machine.

Primitive though such an example is by the **standards** of today, it illustrates the principles of IoT: a "thing" (which could also be a human or animal) is equipped with sensors and wireless technology to transmit information from those sensors over a network to another computer. A thing on IoT could be a person with a heart monitor, concrete in a building, a refrigerator, or a coffee maker. Typically, the thing would send a signal when key conditions were met, such as if the owner of the heart monitor appeared to be having a heart attack, or there was no milk left. In the case of the coffee maker, it might receive a signal, for example from an alarm clock, that someone had woken up and would be wanting coffee soon.

IoT is made possible thanks to the spread of fast wireless networks and the lower costs and accelerated miniaturization of sensors. As with many advances in technology, it appears that many developments are occurring because they are technically possible, without enough attention being given to possible dangers. For example, smart home technology allows a car to contact its owner's home to inform it that the owner will be home soon. The home may turn on the heating in advance and then unlock the door when the owner's cellphone is detected to be in the **vicinity**. If **hacking** allowed someone else to pretend to be the owner, the security risks are clear. People are not only in danger of being **targeted** by criminals. Once IoT is ubiquitous, it will also be possible for governments to engage in constant surveillance of, for example, citizens with **opposing** political views. One report has estimated that, worldwide, there are about 7.3 billion IoT devices that need to be secured urgently.

Another problem for IoT is competing standards. Different companies use different technologies, with the result that it is often impossible for devices to talk to one another.

If these problems can be overcome, IoT could help solve many problems through timely sharing of **key** data. For example, sensors **embedded** in the steel of a bridge or a ship's hull, or in the concrete of a building, could warn of metal fatigue or structural problems, allowing engineers or builders to **intervene** and ₃₅ **ward off** potential disaster. Sensors in forests could warn of very low humidity or high temperatures, allowing **preemptive** action to be taken in forest fire danger zones. The possibilities, many yet to be **envisaged**, promise to change our lives in many ways.

> **NOTES**
>
> **installation** 導入　**savvy** 知識が豊富な　**primitive** 原始的な　**standard** 標準　**vicinity** 近所
> **hacking** ハッキング（コンピュータへの不法侵入）　**target** 〜を標的にする　**opposing** 敵対する
> **key** 極めて重要な　**embedded** 埋め込まれた　**intervene** 介入する　**ward off** 回避する
> **preemptive** 先手を取る　**envisage** 〜と予想する

Comprehension Check

Choose the most suitable answer for each question.

1. What is the relevance of Carnegie Mellon University to the Internet of Things?
   (a) Its IoT department was the first to advocate for the Internet of Things.
   (b) A vending machine at the university does not accept coins, only tokens sent via the Internet.
   (c) A vending machine there was equipped with remotely-accessed sensors in the 1980s.

2. Which of the following is true about IoT?
   (a) It cannot be used with living things.
   (b) It involves transmitting information from sensors over a network.
   (c) It is to be used only in emergencies.

3. Which of the following is NOT true about IoT?
   (a) It involves some security risks.
   (b) Miniaturization is making it more difficult to push IoT forward.
   (c) Some people worry that IoT may make it easier for governments to engage in surveillance.

4. What example of IoT involving a ship is given?
   (a) A sensor embedded in a ship's hull could detect objects such as icebergs.
   (b) Sensors on a ship could remind engineers to perform regular checks of the state of the hull.
   (c) Sensors could detect changes in the condition of the steel in the hull.

Best Summary

From these four sentences, choose the one that summarizes the passage best.

1. The Internet of Things began in the 1980s, thanks to the excellent computing department at Carnegie Mellon University in Pittsburgh.

2. The Internet of Things has lots of potential, but the risks are too great for it to have a future.

3. The Internet of Things involves embedded sensors sending information over wireless networks to another computer. Although there are risks and challenges, there is also great potential.

4. The Internet of Things, which consists of embedded sensors sending information over wireless networks, is overseen by programmers at Carnegie Mellon University in Pittsburgh.

Word Choice

Choose a suitable expression to fill each blank.

1. With IoT, your device could be broadcasting to any number of devices _____.
   (a) in the vicinity   (b) neighboring   (c) to approach   (d) nearness

2. IoT as it is today offers many opportunities to _____ hackers who want to get people's private information.
   (a) savory   (b) foolish   (c) wisdom   (d) savvy

3. Before a security crisis occurs, it is to be hoped that authorities will _____ by creating regulations.
   (a) interfere   (b) intervene   (c) action   (d) escape

4. I have lived with the Internet all my life. It is difficult to _____ life without it.
   (a) illustrate   (b) prohibit   (c) envisage   (d) vision

5. We should not judge current security protocols _____ the 1990s. We should be more demanding.
   (a) looking at   (b) judge by   (c) according to   (d) by the standards of

Composition

Rearrange the words within the parentheses to make sentences.

1. IoT の原理は単純だが、それには深い含蓄がある。

(are / IoT / of / principles / simple / though the), they have profound implications.

_____

2. プライバシーを享受できない未来の可能性を専門家は警告する。

Experts (a / future / of / of / possibility / the / warn / where) we are unable to enjoy any privacy.

_____

3. IoT の長期的な成功のためには、悪人による攻撃を撃退する信頼性のある方法を探すことが必要である。

For the long-term success of IoT, it is necessary (attacks / find / of / off / reliable / to / warding / ways) by bad actors.

_____

4. セキュリティが向上されなければ、IoT は悪評を買う恐れがある。

If security is not improved, IoT (a / bad / danger / getting /in / is / of / reputation).

_____

Partial Dictation and Conversation

🎧 2-14

Listen to the dialogue, and fill in the missing words. Then, speak the dialogue with a partner. After speaking once or twice, switch roles.

A: Do you have any virtual assistants or home automation systems?

B: No. [1] _____ until I have more money! But I'm interested in the technology. I think it has [2] _____.

A: Same here. It would be cool [3] _____ look up a recipe, for example, while cooking [4] _____ use your hands.

B: Did you know that it's also possible to order food delivery with some of those devices, [5] _____ the country?

A: No, I didn't know that.

Active Learning

Look at the chart below, which shows the estimated and projected growth in the Internet of Things. Discuss the topic with a partner, including the questions below.

1. How have things changed since 2012?

2. What was the situation in 2018?

3. What IoT-connected things do you have or do you think it would be good to have?

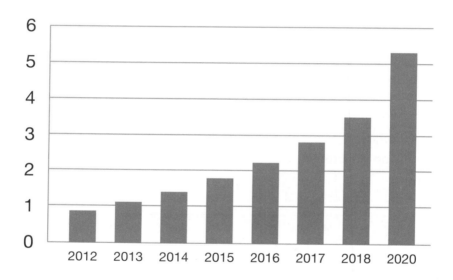

BILLIONS OF CONNECTED DEVICES

[Data sources: https://cerasis.com/iot-supply-chain/
https://hackernoon.com/the-most-promising-internet-of-things-trends-for-2018-10a852ccd189]

WORDS & PHRASES

There has been a rapid increase in _____.
In 2018, the number of devices connected on IoT _____.
Right now, I don't have many IoT devices. But it would be nice to have
_____.

UNIT 13

Easy Payments

電子商取引の世界

現金に頼った取引を見直して、現金を使うことのないキャッシュレス化が進んでいる。国家の方針としてこれを推進している国もあるが、クレジットカードや携帯電話による決済が日本でも浸透していくだろうか。

Vocabulary Preview

Match each word with a definition by drawing a line between them.

1. consumer   •

2. driver   •

3. cash register   •

4. efficiency   •

5. inadequate   •

6. skip   •

7. adoption   •

8. transaction   •

9. utility bill   •

10. accelerate   •

• (a) not enough

• (b) someone who buys goods and services

• (c) to pass over a step or a stage

• (d) a deal

• (e) starting to use a plan or method

• (f) a machine, used in stores, that contains money

• (g) the ability to achieve results without using too many resources

• (h) to make something go faster

• (i) something that has a major influence on a change

• (j) a request or demand to pay for electricity, gas, water, etc.

Electronic payment systems are becoming more and more popular throughout the world. For online shopping, the advantages are obvious. Even in stores, for consumers in general it is seen as more convenient to pay for everything with a single card — or software application or other **identifier** of some kind — than to
5 carry cash around and fish the correct amount out of a pocket or wallet. More than consumer convenience, though, the main driver of the move away from cash is the high cost of building and maintaining a cash **infrastructure**. Printing banknotes and **minting** coins, moving them around the country, setting up bank branches to **cater to** citizens, and installing cash registers in shops all cost money and lower the
10 overall efficiency of national economies.

Countries differ with respect to the speed at which they are moving to electronic payments. For developing nations where cash infrastructure is inadequate, electronic payment systems offer the opportunity to skip at least one stage of development, just as 4G cellphones enabled countries to skip the personal computing revolution and
15 move straight to mobile infrastructure. That may explain the speed of adoption in many African countries.

Sweden is an example of a highly advanced country where cash payments are becoming less and less common. It is calculated that more than 85 percent of transactions are cashless. One reason is that the cold **Nordic** winters make it difficult
20 and costly to move cash around. Another is **presumably** the **progressive** attitude toward most things **prevailing** in Sweden.

In Asia, Vietnam has a rapid reduction in cash transactions as a national goal, aiming to bring the proportion down to 10 percent by 2020. It aims to **digitize** many public services, potentially eliminating cash transactions from hospitals and schools.
25 Many people already pay utility bills electronically. For the time being, to avoid **inconveniencing** people living far away from a bank branch, banks sometimes send employees outside the cities on motorbikes to help customers do their bank transactions.

Also in Asia, there are many different government-backed companies active in
30 the financial sector in the Republic of Korea. This has given rise to a large number of systems that are used for different types of transactions. Korea is already well on its way to becoming a cashless society, and visitors are warned not to rely on cash; a

credit card can be considered a basic necessity.

Japan is generally acknowledged to **lag behind** other high-income countries in its move to electronic payment, perhaps because crime is low and Japanese people feel safe carrying cash. The government engaged in a push to accelerate that movement ahead of the 2020 Tokyo Olympics but with limited success: surveys have found that tourists from overseas are often frustrated at not being able to use their credit cards or get information in advance about whether or not credit card use will be possible. 35

40

NOTES

electronic payment system 電子決済システム **identifier** 識別子 **infrastructure** 社会基盤 **mint** ～を鋳造する **cater to** ～に応じる **Nordic** 北欧（人）の **presumably** 恐らく **progressive** 進歩的な **prevail** 広がる **digitize** ～をデジタル化する **inconvenience** ～に不便を感じさせる **lag behind** 後れを取る

Comprehension Check

Choose the most suitable answer for each question.

1. Which of the following statements is NOT true?
   (a) Cashless payments are useful for both online shopping and for shopping in physical stores.
   (b) In place of a physical card, people sometimes use a software application.
   (c) Consumer convenience is the main reason to switch to a cashless system.

2. Why does the writer think many African countries are quick to adopt cashless systems?
   (a) Their cash infrastructure is underdeveloped.
   (b) They have many personal computers.
   (c) They received 4G systems before other countries did.

3. Which of the following is NOT said about Vietnam?
   (a) It is trying to digitize many public services.
   (b) Bank employees sometimes visit customers outside the cities.
   (c) Most people pay their utility bills in cash.

4. Which of the following is true of the attitude of overseas tourists toward the situation in Japan?
   (a) Crime is very low, so they are happy to use cash.
   (b) They are frustrated at the difficulty of getting information in advance about forms of payment.
   (c) They are worried about their credit cards being stolen.

Best Summary

From these four sentences, choose the one that summarizes the passage best.

1. Electronic payment systems are becoming more common in general but the speed of change is very different from country to country.

2. Japan and the Republic of Korea are slower than other countries to adopt cashless payment systems.

3. There has recently been a pushback against attempts to move to a cashless society.

4. Cashless payment systems require an elaborate infrastructure, making it very difficult for them to spread throughout the world.

Word Choice

Choose a suitable expression to fill each blank.

1. For customers' _____, we offer a large range of payment options.
   (a) easy   (b) helpfulness   (c) convenient   (d) convenience

2. If Japan is unable to cater to international tourists' needs, some of them will _____ visit other countries instead.
   (a) presumably   (b) assuming   (c) probable   (d) likelier

3. A prominent _____ payment system in Japan is e-money cards like Suica.
   (a) no-cash   (b) less-cash   (c) cashless   (d) credited

4. Currently, there is a major government _____ to provide more convenient payment options in Japan.
   (a) encourage   (b) push   (c) hope   (d) hopeful

5. Japan _____ many other countries in terms of payment infrastructure.
   (a) falls out   (b) drops out of   (c) waits out   (d) lags behind

Composition

Rearrange the words within the parentheses to make sentences.

1. 決済システムは必要とされる社会基盤に関して異なる。
   Payment systems differ (infrastructure / require / respect / that / the / they / to / with).

---

2. 経済学者は、利便性が現金に対する愛着を克服するのに十分に強いかどうかを見極めようとしている。

Economists are trying to determine (convenience / enough / is / not / or / strong / whether) to overcome people's attachment to cash.

_____

3. 多くの国の若者は既にもう現金を捨て去るところに近づいている。

Young people in many countries are (abandoning / already / on / their / to / way / well) cash.

_____

4. 日本は当分の間、現金が主体の社会のままでいることが確実視されている。

Japan looks set to remain (a / being / cash-based / for / society / the / time).

_____

Partial Dictation and Conversation　　　　　🎵 2-21

· ·
Listen to the dialogue, and fill in the missing words. Then, speak the dialogue with a partner. After speaking once or twice, switch roles.

A: How close ①_____ to a cashless society?

B: Not very, I would say. ②_____ have a credit card yet.

A: So, you use cash for everything?

B: Well, not exactly. I ③_____to take trains and buses, and I can also use that card at some convenience stores.

A: ④_____ you're moving in a cashless direction.

B: Well, maybe. But in order to "charge" the card with money, I withdraw cash from an ATM and then store that value in the card.
　　⑤_____ cash in the end.

Look at the chart below, which shows the extent to which Americans used cash in 2015 and 2018. Discuss the topic with a partner, including the questions below.

1. How has the percentage of people using cash for all or nearly all purchases changed recently?

2. How about people saying they don't use cash at all?

3. How often do you use non-cash payment? For what kinds of purchases?

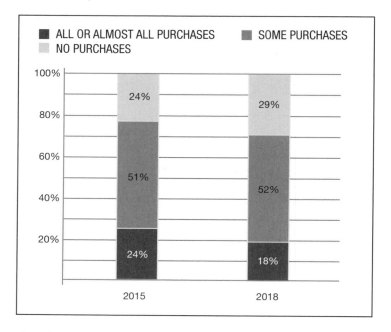

[Data source: https://www.pewresearch.org/fact-tank/2018/12/12/more-americans-are-making-no-weekly-purchases-with-cash/]

WORDS & PHRASES

From 2015 to 2018, the percentage of people who used cash for all or nearly all their purchases _____.
The percentage of people who used cash for none of their purchases, in contrast, _____.
I usually _____.

Let's All Pay
クラウドファンディング

不特定多数の人からインターネット経由で資金調達が容易に行える。ちょっとしたアイデアで提案された様々な分野への投資が少額でも行えるが、多くの支持が得られると多額の資金を得ることが可能である。

Vocabulary Preview

Match each word with a definition by drawing a line between them.

1. speculative
2. niche
3. incentive
4. donate
5. funder
6. delivery
7. notion
8. indie
9. prompt
10. checkbox

(a) a small square on paper or a computer screen

(b) based on guessing

(c) a short form of "independent," often used to refer to movie, music, and software developers

(d) something that encourages people to greater effort

(e) to give something, usually money

(f) the act of taking goods or letters to a place

(g) a signal or encouragement to do something

(h) an idea

(i) an opportunity to provide a product to a small group of customers

(j) a person or organization that gives money for a purpose

The traditional way for a small business to get money to launch a new product is to borrow money from a bank. However, banks may be reluctant to lend money for a speculative idea that may never make money, or to businesses — which in many cases may be a single individual — with no **track record**. For niche ideas, one
5 for which the expected market is very small, **crowdfunding**, made easier thanks to the Internet, is increasingly recognized as a **viable alternative**.

On a crowdfunding site, a business owner can start by pitching an idea to **like-minded** people. If there is little interest, she can give up without making any financial loss; alternatively, she can amend the idea to make it more compelling for
10 other people. Work can start after the funding goal is reached, meaning that the developer does not need to **dig into her own pockets**.

For crowdfunders, the main incentive to donate is that, without donations, the product might never come into existence. In addition, people appreciate being a part of a community where their voices may have some influence on product
15 development. Typically, businesses offer various benefits to funders beyond delivery of the promised product, and larger donors — and sometimes earlier donors — get larger benefits.

Kickstarter, created in 2009, is one of the largest crowdfunding sites, and for many people it is almost **synonymous** with the notion of crowdfunding. Many
20 projects hosted on Kickstarter in those early days were connected with software development. Since the early days of the personal computer, there has been a community of "indie" developers creating shareware. This is software that people can download free of charge and try out for a period, but they are expected to pay for it if they continue to use it. The launch in 2008 of Apple's App Store appears to have
25 created downward pressure on software prices, making life difficult for many of these developers of niche products who needed to charge larger fees per copy of the software. This may be one reason why crowdfunding appealed to such developers.

Of course, crowdfunding is not restricted to software development. One example of a more traditional crowdfunding project is Mind Journal, a business
30 created in the UK by Ollie Aplin, who had suffered emotional problems after the death of his mother. He focused on creating a journal that he felt would have been

just right for him at that time. Aware that men tend not to journal, or give up very soon after starting, he created a journal with lots of questions and various prompts and checkboxes. These reduce the burden of thinking what to write about.

NOTES

track record 実績　**crowdfunding** クラウドファンディング (資金調達の方法の一つで、インターネットなどを通じて多数の支援者やファンから少しずつ資金を集めて目的を達するもの)　**viable** 実行可能な　**alternative** 代替手段　**like-minded** 同じ考えを持った　**dig into one's own pocket** 自分のポケットから取り出す　**synonymous** 同義の

Comprehension Check

Choose the most suitable answer for each question.

1. What reason is given for a business to choose to use crowdfunding?
   (a) The entrepreneur may dislike banks.
   (b) Banks may not want to lend money to some people or for certain ideas.
   (c) It is too much trouble to go to a bank and explain a complex idea.

2. What happens if a business owner cannot find enough people to back a project?
   (a) The owner has to submit a better idea within the time limit.
   (b) The crowdfunding site will take ownership of the business.
   (c) Nothing happens.

3. What benefit to crowdfunders is NOT mentioned?
   (a) They may eventually reform capitalism.
   (b) They may like being part of a community.
   (c) They may get some special benefits.

4. What prompted the launch of Mind Journal?
   (a) The owner wanted help to pay his mother's hospital bills.
   (b) The death of the owner's mother.
   (c) The presence of too many checkboxes in traditional journals.

Best Summary

From these four sentences, choose the one that summarizes the passage best.

1. Mind Journal is a good template for those considering starting a crowdfunding project.

2. Because of various problems with the technical infrastructure, crowdfunding projects do not usually go very well.

3. Crowdfunding is becoming increasingly popular for niche products.

4. Kickstarter and Apple have grown steadily in size to become the biggest crowdfunding companies.

Word Choice

Choose a suitable expression to fill each blank.

1. Entry is _____ those over 18.
   (a) conflicted to   (b) limited at   (c) restricted to   (d) delimited by

2. Crowdfunding has the advantage for entrepreneurs that banks don't have any _____ what products should be created.
   (a) power on   (b) rights of   (c) influence to   (d) influence on

3. For many people, Silicon Valley is _____ high tech.
   (a) synonymous with   (b) similar to   (c) reminding   (d) imaging

4. It is expected that products _____ the environment or health will become more numerous.
   (a) linked in   (b) connected with   (c) relating   (d) related

5. Many governments are trying to _____ taxation on entrepreneurs.
   (a) reduce the burden of   (b) ease the weight on
   (c) lighten the responsibility   (d) give up to

Composition

Rearrange the words within the parentheses to make sentences.

1. クラウドファンディングは21世紀初めに出現した。
   Crowdfunding (came / century / early / existence / in / into / the / 21st).

   _____

2. 銀行は実績のない起業家にお金を貸したがらない。

Banks (lend / like to / money / not / tend / to / to entrepreneurs / without) a track record.

_____

3. 購読モデルでは、毎月あるいは毎年ソフトウェアの代金を支払うことを要求される。

In a subscription model, people (are / expected / every / for / month / pay / software / to) or year.

_____

4. クラウドファンディングのプロジェクトに寄付を申し出るときに、その製品が完成するわけではないかもしれないことを知っていることは重要である。

When pledging money to a crowdfunded project, it is important to (aware / be / be / completed / may / never / that / the product).

_____

Partial Dictation and Conversation

🎧 2-27

Listen to the dialogue, and fill in the missing words. Then, speak the dialogue with a partner. After speaking once or twice, switch roles.

A: Have you ever tried a crowdfunding site?

B: What's that?

A: ☐1 _____ crowdfunding? You can describe your business idea on a special website and say ☐2 _____ to realize the idea. If the money is raised, you go ahead with the project. The people who pledged money usually get some kind of special reward.

B: ☐3 _____ for business people. But I'm still a student!

A: Fair enough. But in countries like the UK and the U.S., ☐4 _____, some students are crowdfunding their education. And some graduate students ☐5 _____ are crowdfunding their research!

B: Really? That's difficult to imagine.

Look at the chart, which shows the amount of money pledged each year on the well-known crowdfunding site Kickstarter. Talk about the data with a partner, including the following questions.

1. How has the popularity of Kickstarter changed since 2009?

2. How successful do you expect crowdfunding to be in the future?

3. What do you think of the idea of crowdfunding?

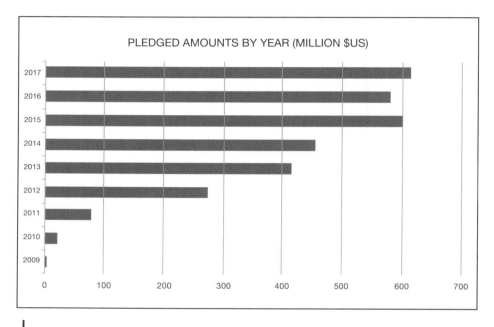

PLEDGED AMOUNTS BY YEAR (MILLION $US)

[Data source: http://icopartners.com/2018/01/kickstarter-2017-year-review/]

⬛ WORDS & PHRASES

The graph shows a rapid rise in dollars pledged until 2015, when it reached _____.

There was a slight drop in _____, followed by a slight rise _____.

I think it is _____.

Where Do You Want to Fly Today?

空飛ぶクルマ

車は一般的で便利なものであるが、環境面のコストなどが問題と考えられる。空飛ぶクルマは次世代の移動手段として期待されるが、その実現までには解決しなければならないことがある。

Vocabulary Preview

Match each word with a definition by drawing a line between them.

1. pollution ● ● (a) being unable to do something

2. infrastructure ● ● (b) the systems that enable things to work

3. congestion ● ● (c) processes or substances that damage the environment

4. advantage ● ● (d) to keep away from, or prevent

5. vehicle ● ● (e) activities that people do to enjoy themselves

6. promotional ● ● (f) difficulty in moving around because of crowding

7. leisure ● ● (g) a benefit

8. inability ● ● (h) a machine used to move people or things

9. concept ● ● (i) an idea

10. avoid ● ● (j) related to advertising

Cars are so popular because, **by and large**, they meet our needs. We can jump in whenever we want and just drive wherever we want to go. But they come with their own **costs**, air pollution among them. Add to the list the costs, not only environmental, of creating the driving and parking infrastructure required by cars.

5 And besides, when congestion gets too bad, cars are no longer even very good at their **primary** purpose: getting us where we need to go.

For very long trips, airplanes are the only way to get around fast, despite their environmental costs. They are not really viable, however, for shorter trips, since the effort required to get to an airport, check in, and wait for flights is too much. This is

10 where flying cars may come in. **In theory**, they may combine the advantages of the personal car and of airplanes.

One of the many products that are likely to be available soon is the BlackFly, from California-based Opener. A **vertical take-off and landing vehicle** for a single person, it is designed to fly short trips of up to 25 miles. It can take off and land on

15 sea and land. It also has a function that assists take-off and landing, so the operator does not need a pilot's license. Prices have not yet been announced, but it is likely to cost around the same as an **SUV**.

BlackFly promotional **materials** show young people on camping or adventure trips in the countryside, with no-one else in sight, suggesting that the product is

20 aimed mainly at the leisure market. Its inability to carry more than one person and low **range** limit its ability to replace the family car. One vehicle that promises to overcome these limitations is the Volante Vision, from Aston Martin. Although currently just a concept vehicle, the Volante Vision holds three people and is designed for **inter-city** travel.

25 Vehicles larger and more powerful than the BlackFly are likely to be **prohibitively** expensive for individual buyers. Therefore, companies like Lilium Aviation from Germany and Uber, the California-based company already well-known in Japan and in many other countries, are working on the concept of air taxis. As they see it, there is no need for everyone to own their own vehicle if use of a vehicle is readily

30 and widely available at a **reasonable** cost.

For flying cars to be a success, there are still a lot of issues to be worked out

— not least safety considerations such as how to avoid **in-air collisions**, which are much more likely to be deadly than on the roads. But surveying the technological **offerings**, it is difficult not to conclude that air travel will soon be part of our daily lives.

35

NOTES

by and large 概して   **cost** 代償   **primary** 主な   **in theory** 理論的には   **vertical take-off and landing vehicle** 垂直離着陸機   **SUV** (sport utility vehicle) スポーツ用多目的車   **material** 資料   **range** 航続距離   **inter-city** 都市間の   **prohibitively** とてつもなく   **reasonable** 手頃な   **in-air collision** 空中衝突   **offering** 提供されるもの

Comprehension Check

Choose the most suitable answer for each question.

1. Which disadvantage of private cars is NOT mentioned?
   (a) Building roads is expensive.
   (b) Cars contribute to global warming.
   (c) Traffic jams sometimes make cars inconvenient.

2. Which problem with conventional airplanes is mentioned?
   (a) The time spent before flying is excessive.
   (b) The risk of accidents is high.
   (c) They are not good for very long trips.

3. How viable is the BlackFly as a replacement for the family car?
   (a) If the cost is lowered it could be ideal.
   (b) It is good for trips in town but not for the mountains.
   (c) It holds only one person, so it is not viable.

4. Which of the following is true?
   (a) The Volante Vision is now widely available.
   (b) The Volante Vision has a greater range than the BlackFly.
   (c) The Volante Vision can carry a large family.

From these four sentences, choose the one that summarizes the passage best.

1. There are many interesting flying vehicle prototypes, including the BlackFly and the Volante Vision, but their short range and environmental costs mean that they are unlikely to be useful.

2. Conventional cars are generally convenient, but traffic congestion means that flying cars are likely to become more popular for longer trips.

3. Although current flying cars have various limitations, such as high prices and short ranges, it seems likely that they will become part of our lives in the near future.

4. Flying cars are now perfectly safe for anyone to use, so it seems likely that they will replace conventional cars and airplanes very soon.

~~~ Word Choice ~~~

Choose a suitable expression to fill each blank.

1. One vehicle from Opener is _____ to transport one person over short distances.
   (a) aimed   (b) designed   (c) arranging   (d) requested

2. Airplanes are _____ only for longer trips.
   (a) potential   (b) exciting   (c) viable   (d) powerful

3. The BlackFly is aimed mainly at the _____ market.
   (a) militaristic   (b) busy   (c) professionally   (d) leisure

4. We need to _____ a lot of issues before flying cars become popular.
   (a) work out   (b) drive through   (c) think out   (d) succeed

5. Probably, air travel will _____ be part of our daily lives.
   (a) conclusively   (b) soon   (c) eventual   (d) ever

~~~ Composition ~~~

Rearrange the words within the parentheses to make sentences.

1. 空飛ぶ車は将来もっと一般的になるかもしれないが、従来の車を売ってしまう必要はまだない。

   Flying cars may become more common in the future, but there (for / is / need / no / sell / to / you) your conventional car yet.

2. 空飛ぶタクシーの導入を考えている会社もある。これはそのコンセプトが実行可能なものであるという考えを示す。

Some companies are thinking about introducing air taxis, (be / concept / could / suggesting / that / the / they / think) a viable one.

_____

3. 空飛ぶ車が大量生産品として成功するには、価格が相当に下がらなければならない。

For (a / as / cars / flying / it / make / to) mass-market product category, prices are going to have to come down considerably.

_____

4. 交通渋滞の大きな経済負担を考慮すると、公共交通により大きな投資が必要だと結論づけざるを得ない。

Considering the massive economic costs of traffic congestion, (conclude / difficult / is / it / not / that / to) public transportation needs greater investment.

_____

Partial Dictation and Conversation
🎧 2-34

Listen to the dialogue, and fill in the missing words. Then, speak the dialogue with a partner. After speaking once or twice, switch roles.

A: Hey, did you see the documentary last night?

B: You mean ① _____ flying vehicles? Yes, I saw that, too.

A: Well, what did you think?

B: I don't know. It's interesting but I don't think it's ② _____ important topic at this time. It's probably more important to ③ _____ public transportation.

A: ④ _____. In a lot of countries, the use of cars is still increasing, bringing lots of problems like air pollution and congestion.

B: Yes. Once the roads get congested, the advantages of cars all disappear. We should have more buses or trams, and improve rail systems. We ⑤ _____ boosting the use of bikes.

Active Learning

Look at the graph below, which shows changes in car sharing in Japan from 2002 to 2017. With a partner, describe the trends and discuss possible reasons, including these questions.

1. What was the situation with car sharing in Japan in 2011?

2. How has the situation changed since then?

3. What do you think of car sharing?

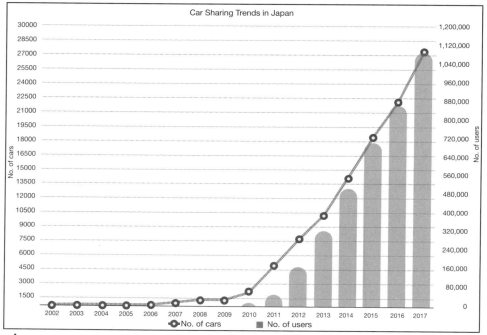

[Data sources: https://www.sg.kyoto-u.ac.jp/jp/pdf/programme/researchpaper/2017/01.pdf
http://www.ecomo.or.jp/environment/carshare/carshare_graph2018.3.html]

WORDS & PHRASES

The most obvious thing is that _____.
There has been a (rapid/steady) increase (in _____) since _____
_____ surpassed 1 million in _____.
I think it _____.

Flying Tonight

これからの月面開発

月面の無人探査、そして月面へ人類を送ることが目標となっている。そのミッションは月面に基地を造って人類が生活して、月面探査を行い、他の天体の探査の足がかりにすることである。

Vocabulary Preview

Match each word with a definition by drawing a line between them.

1. mission   •
2. feasible   •
3. permanently   •
4. sustainability   •
5. initiative   •
6. successor   •
7. hospitable   •
8. geology   •
9. shield   •
10. hub   •

• (a) rocks and other substances that make up a planet's surface

• (b) welcoming toward visitors

• (c) likely to be achieved

• (d) an important official job given to a person or group of people

• (e) for a long time, forever

• (f) someone or something that takes over a position from someone/something else

• (g) the ability to continue or be continued for a long time

• (h) a key place for an activity

• (i) an important plan or process

• (j) to protect someone or something from harm

Human **exploration** of the Moon began in 1969 with the Apollo 11 mission, which famously landed Neil Armstrong and Buzz Aldrin there, and ended in 1972 with the Apollo 17 mission. By then, the American public's **fascination with** space had cooled **considerably**, and the government was concerned about spending
5 billions of dollars on a program with few obvious returns on investment.

The work of the **National Aeronautic and Space Administration (NASA)** since that time has tended to focus on **unmanned** exploration of space. But an announcement from U.S. President Donald Trump in 2017 has established a return of humans to the Moon as a key goal.

10 One reason why it may be feasible **eventually** for humans to live permanently on the Moon is that its surface appears to have billions of tons of water ice. If a base were constructed near the **lunar South Pole**, where sunlight is nearly constant, large amounts of solar power could be generated. This could be used to melt the ice for drinking water and also to split the water into oxygen for people to breathe and
15 hydrogen to use for fuel.

Interest in such aspects of a possible base reflect a general concern with sustainability of future space initiatives, in contrast with earlier programs such as the Apollo program. Another hopeful sign is that research has shown that carrots and tomatoes can grow in soil similar to that found on the Moon.

20 One reason for the high cost of many missions is the difficulty of escaping the Earth's **gravitational pull**. The **International Space Station** — or its successors — create the potential for launching missions from low Earth orbit, eliminating most of that cost. If current U.S. plans are carried out, a similar station in lunar orbit will allow one kind of spaceship to travel between the space stations and another kind to
25 travel between the lunar station and the lunar surface.

It is well known that the Moon's atmosphere is extremely thin. The surface is rocky and dusty and it experiences extremes of heat and cold; it is not a hospitable place for humans. Nevertheless, scientists point to a number of advantages of returning to the Moon. A major one is scientific: we will be able to continue the
30 exploration of the Moon's geology at an accelerated pace, and this will give us more information about the Earth and the history of the universe. In addition, the far

side of the Moon is shielded from **radio interference** coming from the Earth and can therefore provide a good site for **astronomical** research. Scientists also mention mining and even using the Moon as a manufacturing hub. Having much weaker gravity than the Earth, the Moon is also a better base for exploring Mars and further 35 afield.

NOTES

exploration 探査　**fascination with** 〜に感じている魅力　**considerably** 大幅に **National Aeronautic and Space Administration** アメリカ航空宇宙局（**NASA**）**unmanned** 無人の **eventually** 最終的に　**lunar South Pole** 月の南極　**gravitational pull** 引力 **International Space Station** 国際宇宙ステーション　**radio interference** 無線妨害 **astronomical** 天文学の

Comprehension Check

Choose the most suitable answer for each question.

1. Who were the first people to walk on the Moon, and when did they do it?
   (a) Buzz Aldrin and Neil Armstrong walked on the Moon in 1969.
   (b) The Apollo 17 astronauts were the first, in 1969.
   (c) Neil Armstrong did it in 1972.

2. Why are there renewed efforts to send humans to the Moon?
   (a) NASA does not like unmanned flights.
   (b) The U.S. president stipulated that as a goal.
   (c) Political leaders are worried about the high cost of the robots used on unmanned flights.

3. What is likely to be a good place to site a permanent lunar base, and why?
   (a) The lunar North Pole is good because it has lots of sunlight.
   (b) It would be best to explore the lunar surface in order to find somewhere that has ice.
   (c) The lunar South Pole is a promising site because lots of solar power could be generated there.

4. What is a likely advantage of using a space station in orbit?
   (a) It can be used to build a chain of space stations.
   (b) It would allow astronauts to maintain the space station at the same time as carrying out a lunar mission.
   (c) It would lower the costs of escaping the gravitational pull of the Earth.

From these four sentences, choose the one that summarizes the passage best.

1. The Moon is comparatively easy to get to, so it is probable that there will be permanent human settlements on the Moon very soon.

2. Renewed interest in sending humans to the Moon may eventually lead to human settlements there.

3. A lack of raw materials on the Earth will soon lead to mining on the Moon.

4. The American public has gradually lost interest in the Moon, but believes that NASA should send astronauts there regularly.

Word Choice

Choose a suitable expression to fill each blank.

1. Studies of the _____ of the Moon will help researchers to decide whether mining is viable there.
   (a) geology   (b) physiology   (c) psychology   (d) anthropology

2. The fact that the far side of the Moon is shielded from radio interference coming from the Earth is _____ for astronomers.
   (a) a puzzle   (b) problematic   (c) an advantage   (d) a disadvantage

3. One NASA _____ involves constructing a kind of space station in lunar orbit.
   (a) intuition   (b) inconvenience   (c) inspiration   (d) initiative

4. One _____ requirement for any long-term presence on the Moon is access to water.
   (a) clearly   (b) obvious   (c) evidence   (d) growing

5. It is _____ easier to get to the Moon than to Mars.
   (a) very   (b) considerably   (c) extremely   (d) considerately

Composition

Rearrange the words within the parentheses to make sentences.

1. 人々の月に感じている魅力は数十万年前にさかのぼる。
   People's (back / fascination / goes / of / the Moon / hundreds of thousands / with / years).

2. 地球が太陽と月の間にあるときに皆既月食が起こるのはよく知られている。

It (a / occurs / eclipse / is / total lunar / that / well-known / when) the Earth is between the Sun and the Moon.

_____

3. 私は、人類が宇宙探査を諦める可能性に憂慮している。

I am (about / concerned / give / humans / that / the possibility / up / will) exploring space.

_____

4. アポロ計画は、ソビエト連邦を打ち負かすことに関するアメリカ政府の関心を反映した。

The design (Apollo program / beating the / general concern / of the / reflected / the / U.S. government's / with) Soviet Union.

_____

Partial Dictation and Conversation 🎧 2-41

Listen to the dialogue, and fill in the missing words. Then, speak the dialogue with a partner. After speaking once or twice, switch roles.

A: Do you know much about NASA?

B: Well, ① _____, but my parents have told me a bit about the Apollo missions. They used to watch them on TV.

A: Ah, yes, I heard ② _____ about the Apollo 11 mission, when humans first walked on the Moon.

B: There was a movie about that, ③ _____?

A: Oh, yes, I know the one you mean: *First Man*. It ④ _____ in 2018.

B: What's a bit weird is that, after a few more missions over the next few years, ⑤ _____ to the Moon.

A: Yes, that is a bit weird, isn't it?

Active Learning ➤

Look at the timeline, which shows missions to the Moon since 1959. Talk about the data with a partner, including the following questions.

1. When was the first successful mission to the Moon?
2. What happened in 1969?
3. When was the last Apollo mission?

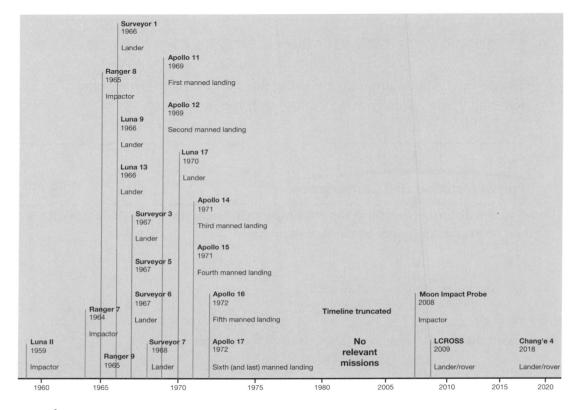

[Data source: https://en.wikipedia.org/wiki/List_of_missions_to_the_Moon]

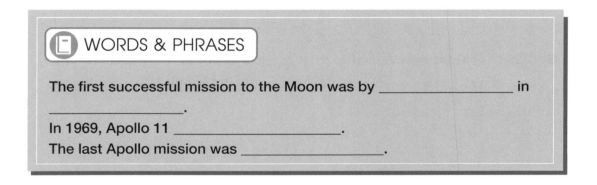

WORDS & PHRASES

The first successful mission to the Moon was by _____ in
_____.

In 1969, Apollo 11 _____.

The last Apollo mission was _____.

UNIT 17

Off to the Asteroids

ハヤブサの偉業

日本の JAXA が行っているハヤブサのミッションは小惑星の標本を地球に持ち帰ることである。それを基に太陽系の歴史を知ることが期待されている。ハヤブサ 2 が小惑星で行ったミッションはどのようなものだったのか。

Vocabulary Preview

Match each word with a definition by drawing a line between them.

1. prominent ●
2. asteroid ●
3. footage ●
4. malfunction ●
5. maneuver ●
6. debris ●
7. rover ●
8. capsule ●
9. analyze ●
10. exhaust ●

● (a) to examine something carefully

● (b) well-known and important

● (c) a small vehicle, often remotely controlled or self-driving

● (d) part of a spacecraft used to hold people or important cargo

● (e) pieces of something left over after it is smashed

● (f) to use all there is of something

● (g) a fault in the way something works

● (h) a skillful or careful movement

● (i) film that keeps a record of an event

● (j) a large rock that circles the sun

Hayabusa and Hayabusa2 are two prominent missions of the **Japanese Aerospace Exploration Agency** (JAXA). The first Hayabusa mission visited the asteroid Itokawa and returned samples of it to the Earth in 2010. Hayabusa2 is investigating another asteroid, Ryugu.

5　　　Asteroids are important targets of exploration, since they are some of the oldest **bodies** in the Solar System and not subject to the same changes experienced by the Earth's surface. Information obtained from them is useful in learning about the history of the Solar System.

　　　The Hayabusa missions have captured the imagination of the Japanese people.
10 The project website shows still and moving images of some of the explorers' operations, as well as footage of the project scientists monitoring the missions. Hayabusa experienced several malfunctions and unexpected problems but made a **near-miraculous** return to the Earth. Hayabusa2 has performed an interesting **sequence** of maneuvers, touching down to collect surface material, then taking off
15 and **firing** a large **copper impactor** (or "**bullet**") into the asteroid to create a **crater**. While the bullet was on its way to the surface, the explorer moved away to the other side of the asteroid to escape debris from the impact, and then, in April 2019, returned to near the surface to observe the crater. In this way, it was possible to get data not only on the surface but also on the **composition** of the asteroid below the surface.

20　　　Hayabusa2 has rovers that it sends out to collect rocks. Because the surface gravity is very weak, the rovers would float upwards if attempting to move around on wheels, so instead they hop around. Each hop takes the rover up to 15 meters into the air and then back down to the surface within 15 minutes. Photos from the surface and also from the air have been transmitted back to the Earth and shown on
25 the project website, enabling the public to keep up with recent developments.

　　　Samples collected from Ryugu are stored in the explorer's sample-return capsule. When Hayabusa2 returns to the vicinity of the Earth, it will release the capsule, which will re-enter the Earth's atmosphere. It is scheduled to land in Australia, after which the samples will be analyzed at a JAXA facility. As for Hayabusa2 itself, its
30 mission may still not be over. It is expected to still hold significant amounts of fuel, so it may be directed to another asteroid for a **flyby** observation.

Whether the data collected by Hayabusa2 will be of more than scientific interest is **yet to** be determined, but there is **speculation** that Ryugu and other similar asteroids could contain billions of dollars' worth of **precious** metals and other construction materials. With many materials necessary for modern industry likely 35 to be exhausted on the Earth within a few decades, this is a matter of **keen** interest to many companies.

> **NOTES**
>
> **Japanese Aerospace Exploration Agency** 宇宙航空研究開発機構　**body** 天体
> **near-miraculous** ほとんど奇跡的な　**sequence** 連続　**fire** 〜を発射する　**copper** 銅
> **impactor** 衝突体　**bullet** 弾丸　**crater** 隕石孔、クレーター　**composition** 組成
> **flyby** 接近通過（天体を観測する目的で接近するが、着陸せずに通過すること）　**yet to** いまだ〜
> されない　**speculation** 推論　**precious** 貴重な　**keen** 強い

Comprehension Check

Choose the most suitable answer for each question.

1. What are Hayabusa and Hayabusa2?
   (a) They are space missions, one of them run by JAXA.
   (b) They are two space missions, run by JAXA, aimed at investigating asteroids.
   (c) They are two missions sent to investigate the asteroid Ryugu.

2. Which of the following statements is NOT true?
   (a) Asteroids are very old.
   (b) The Hayabusa website sometimes shows photos or videos of the missions.
   (c) The Hayabusa mission went very smoothly.

3. What kind of operation undertaken by Hayabusa2 is described?
   (a) After collecting surface material, it shot a kind of bullet into Ryugu to create a crater.
   (b) It flew away from the asteroid when it detected an earthquake.
   (c) A malfunction prevented it from carrying out any operations.

4. Which of the following statements is true?
   (a) Companies have begun mining Ryugu.
   (b) Ryugu is interesting from a scientific point of view, but does not have anything of monetary value.
   (c) Many companies hope that some asteroids contain valuable materials.

Best Summary

From these four sentences, choose the one that summarizes the passage best.

1. The main contribution of the Hayabusa missions is that it found useful resources, such as precious materials, on asteroids.

2. The Hayabusa missions have led to the development of hopping rovers that will be useful in many future missions.

3. The Hayabusa missions have shown that it is possible to perform complex maneuvers in space.

4. The two Hayabusa missions are helping scientists to learn more about asteroids.

Word Choice

Choose a suitable expression to fill each blank.

1. Just like the earlier Apollo missions, the Hayabusa missions have _____ people's imagination.
   (a) imprisoned   (b) captured   (c) entrapped   (d) given

2. Although unmanned missions to asteroids are not as spectacular as manned missions to the Moon, they _____ lots of valuable data.
   (a) gave   (b) overcome   (c) obtain   (d) are given

3. Many asteroids _____ to contain precious metals.
   (a) expect   (b) are expected   (c) are experienced   (d) are determined

4. It is hoped that _____ metals may be abundant in the asteroids.
   (a) worthwhile   (b) expensive   (c) analyzed   (d) precious

5. The results of the Hayabusa2 mission are a matter of _____ interest to many people.
   (a) practicable   (b) sharp   (c) keen   (d) immensely

Composition

Rearrange the words within the parentheses to make sentences.

1. 宇宙探査ミッションは一般的に、始まった後でさえ変更される可能性がある。
   Space missions are generally (after / change / even / have / subject / they / to) begun.

2. ハヤブサは元々は 2002 年 7 月に打ち上げる予定だった。

   Hayabusa (in / July / launch / originally / scheduled / to / was), 2002.

   _____

3. ハヤブサやハヤブサ 2 のようなミッションはどのようにして太陽系が形成されたのかを私たちが知るのを可能にするかもしれない。

   Missions like Hayabusa and Hayabusa2 (enable / find / how / may / out / to / us) the Solar System was formed.

   _____

4. 鉱物を求めて小惑星を採掘することが採算の合うことかどうかいまだ確定されていない。

   It is (asteroids / be / determined / for / mining / to / whether / yet) minerals will be economically viable.

   _____

Partial Dictation and Conversation

🎧 2-48

Listen to the dialogue, and fill in the missing words. Then, speak the dialogue with a partner. After speaking once or twice, switch roles.

A: Are you interested in asteroids?

B: Well, I've played an asteroid video game. I had to mine asteroids and deliver goods to various planets, while ① _____ by an asteroid.

A: Oh, that sounds exciting, but not very realistic! Asteroids are spread across ② _____ of space, so you are very unlikely to be hit by one. And ③ _____ an asteroid sounds like crazy science fiction!

B: Well, you may be right about ④ _____ getting hit by an asteroid. But a lot of companies are looking into the possibilities of mining asteroids, and they've been analyzing their composition and calculating how much money they could make by mining each one.

A: Wow, I never knew that. ⑤ _____.

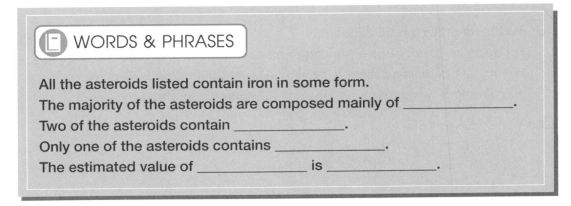

Active Learning

Look at the table below, which shows the 10 asteroids to which it is considered most cost-effective to plan a mining mission. (This judgment reflects not only the value of the substances but the cost of mounting a mission, which depends largely on the path of the asteroid and its distance from the Earth.) With a partner, talk about the data, including the following questions.

1. What substances are present in the asteroids shown?

2. Which asteroids are estimated to have the most value?

3. From which asteroid could platinum be obtained?

NAME	ESTIMATED VALUE (US $ MILLION)	COMPOSITION
Ryugu	82,760	nickel, iron, cobalt
1989 ML	13,940	nickel, iron, cobalt
Nereus	4,710	nickel, iron, cobalt
Bennu	670	iron
Didymos	62,250	nickel, iron, cobalt
2011 UW158	6,690	platinum, nickel, iron, cobalt
Anteros	5,570,000	magnesium silicate, aluminum, iron silicate
2001 CC21	147,040	magnesium silicate, aluminum, iron silicate
1992 TC	84,010	nickel, iron, cobalt
2001 SG10	3,050	nickel, iron, cobalt

[Data source: https://www.asterank.com/]

WORDS & PHRASES

All the asteroids listed contain iron in some form.
The majority of the asteroids are composed mainly of _____.
Two of the asteroids contain _____.
Only one of the asteroids contains _____.
The estimated value of _____ is _____.

UNIT 18 Going Beyond
宇宙開発競争

従来、宇宙は政府機関が主導的に関心を持ち、民間業者の協力を得ていた。近年では、民間企業が宇宙の分野に参入して大型ロケットの開発を行い、政府機関の委託を受けたり独自の事業に取り組んでいる。今後の動向が注目される。

Vocabulary Preview

Match each word with a definition by drawing a line between them.

1. equivalent (n.) •
2. private •
3. contractor •
4. wealthy •
5. equipment •
6. satellite •
7. fuel •
8. rivalry •
9. pioneer •
10. visionary •

• (a) a substance used to power a machine
• (b) something that has the same qualities or function
• (c) imaginative and clear
• (d) having a lot of money
• (e) an electronic device that goes around a planet or other body
• (f) a person or company that agrees to do work for another
• (g) one of the first people to do something new
• (h) not public; related to an individual or a company
• (i) a set of tools and clothes used for a particular purpose
• (j) a situation in which people, companies, or teams compete with one another

Space has traditionally been primarily the concern of governmental organizations such as the U.S.'s National Aeronautics and Space Administration (NASA) and its Russian, Chinese, Indian, European, and Japanese equivalents. (Many other countries have space agencies, but their **capabilities** are limited.)
5 Private companies have long been involved, but generally as contractors. For a number of years, though, a number of private companies with wealthy owners have been becoming more **prominent** in space.

Elon Musk, the founder of the Tesla car company, owns another company called SpaceX. That company has a powerful rocket called the Falcon Heavy, which is often
10 put to use carrying equipment for NASA and other agencies. But **landing** government contracts is not the company's **ultimate** goal. Recently, it has sent satellites into orbit as part of a plan to set up a better broadband Internet service on the Earth.

Since NASA's plans are **vulnerable** to the changing moods of politicians and U.S. government budgets, commercial companies may have important roles to play,
15 and those with **billionaire** owners may have the advantage of more **stable** funding. Another billionaire-owned company is Blue Origin, launched by Amazon owner Jeff Bezos. As with SpaceX, a key goal is to make space flight much more **affordable** and reliable than it has been so far. Blue Origin has achieved several successful test flights of its New Shepard rockets.

20 Another billionaire with a space company is Richard Branson of Virgin Atlantic and Virgin Records fame, with Virgin Galactic. Virgin Galactic has also launched its SpaceShipTwo models successfully into **outer space**. Virgin Galactic, too, emphasizes affordable and reliable space travel, which the company plans to make available to people other than professional astronauts. Virgin Galactic's approach to spaceship
25 launches is to use a large airplane to carry the spaceship high into the air. That means the spaceship does not need the large amount of fuel usually needed to escape the land.

The term "space race" used to mean just one part of the **high-stakes superpower** rivalry of the Soviet Union and the United States, which was also played out on the
30 sea and on land. The Soviet Union was the first country to put a human into outer space, after which the U.S. was the first country to put humans on the Moon. Now,

when people like Elon Musk refer to the space race, they mean this rather friendlier rivalry between different companies.

The three companies mentioned are not the only ones involved with space. A company called Planetary Resources is developing technologies to enable asteroid 35 mining, potentially solving future resource shortages. Many of the company founders have a strong vision of humans as explorers and pioneers, and a belief that we should not be focused only on solving practical short-term problems but hold ambitious and visionary goals as a species.

> **NOTES**
>
> **capability** 能力　**prominent** 目立つ　**land** 〜を獲得する　**ultimate** 最終的な
> **vulnerable** 脆弱な、脆い　**billionaire** 億万長者　**stable** 安定した　**affordable** 手頃な料金
> の　**outer space** 宇宙空間　**high-stakes** いちかばちかの　**superpower** 超大国

Comprehension Check

Choose the most suitable answer for each question.

1. What notable change in space exploration is mentioned near the beginning of the passage?
   (a) The U.S. is losing to China, Russia, and some other countries.
   (b) Private companies now prefer to work as contractors.
   (c) Private companies have started to do their own work in space.

2. What has SpaceX been doing recently, excluding contract work?
   (a) It has been sending satellites into orbit in order to make a better broadband Internet service.
   (b) It has been trying to improve the Falcon Heavy.
   (c) It has been working with Blue Origin.

3. What are the space companies of Richard Branson and Jeff Bezos, respectively?
   (a) Blue Origin and Virgin Atlantic
   (b) New Shepard and Virgin Galactic
   (c) Virgin Galactic and Blue Origin

4. What does the term "space race" mean these days?
   (a) It refers to the rivalry between the U.S. and Russia.
   (b) It refers to a commercial rivalry between space companies.
   (c) It refers to the rivalry between the U.S. and China.

Best Summary

From these four sentences, choose the one that summarizes the passage best.

1. The new space race involves private companies, rather than governments, seeking ways to make a profit in space.

2. The future of space exploration lies in innovative rockets such as New Shepard and Falcon Heavy.

3. Rivalry between the superpowers is likely to continue to be the main feature of space exploration.

4. Mankind will fulfill its destiny by going to the Moon and to Mars, and eventually to the rest of the Solar System.

Word Choice

Choose a suitable expression to fill each blank.

1. Private companies _____ SpaceX and Blue Origin are arguably leading the space race.
   (a) as   (b) like as   (c) ex.   (d) such as

2. Space exploration may allow us to avoid resource _____ in the future.
   (a) lack   (b) lacking   (c) short of   (d) shortages

3. Many kinds of companies are now _____ space exploration, whether directly or indirectly.
   (a) involving   (b) involved with   (c) dealing   (d) dealing to

4. The race to find ways of mining materials off-world could in future become a _____ business.
   (a) expensive-bet   (b) low-dealing   (c) high-stakes   (d) throughout

5. There are plans to send humans to the Moon again, _____ missions to Mars are planned.
   (a) after which   (b) after what   (c) after that time   (d) after when

Composition

Rearrange the words within the parentheses to make sentences.

1. 少数の会社が小惑星の採掘を商業的に実現可能にしようと力を尽くしている。
   A few companies are (asteroid / commercially / make / mining / to / viable / working).

2. どの国が最初に人間を火星に送ることになるのか推測するのは興味深い。

It is interesting to speculate what country will (a / be / first / human / send / the / to / to) Mars.

_____

3. 宇宙競争に携わっている民間企業は発見したものに関する情報を一般市民に入手できるようにすることが期待される。

It is to be hoped that private companies engaged in the space race will (about / available / discoveries / information / make / their / to) the general public.

_____

4. 無重力の中で生活する宇宙飛行士は筋力低下を起こしやすい。

Astronauts (become / gravity / living / in / low / to/ vulnerable) loss of muscle strength.

_____

Partial Dictation and Conversation

CD 2-55

Listen to the dialogue, and fill in the missing words. Then, speak the dialogue with a partner. After speaking once or twice, switch roles.

A: Would you like to go into space?

B: I've never thought about it, really. It doesn't ①_____ happen in my lifetime.

A: Well, I wonder. Some private companies have made commercial spaceships, and ②_____ to bring prices down. They want to make it possible for ordinary people to go into space.

B: It sounds ③_____, but what is the purpose of going? Is it just curiosity?

A: Well, yeah, I guess. But the global space economy is growing, so some people may need to go ④_____.

B: I guess. Maybe we should also learn Martian as well as English — ⑤_____. Is it offered in our curriculum?

Look at the chart below, which shows the approximate value of the various sectors of the global space economy, most based around satellites. Talk about the data with a partner.

1. What was the total value of the global space economy calculated to be in 2017?

2. What are the biggest sectors of that economy?

3. What is the value of the launch industry?

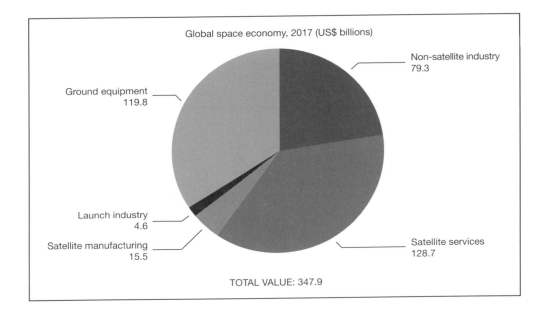

Global space economy, 2017 (US$ billions)

Non-satellite industry 79.3

Ground equipment 119.8

Launch industry 4.6

Satellite manufacturing 15.5

Satellite services 128.7

TOTAL VALUE: 347.9

[Data source:https://www.sia.org/wp-content/uploads/2018/06/2018-SSIR-2-Pager-.pdf]

WORDS & PHRASES

The total value of the global space economy in 2017 _____.

The largest sector _____ and the second largest sector _____.

Other sectors are _____, which has a value of _____,

and _____, which has _____.

UNIT 19

The Red Planet

火星の魅力

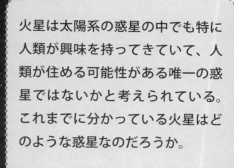

火星は太陽系の惑星の中でも特に人類が興味を持ってきていて、人類が住める可能性がある唯一の惑星ではないかと考えられている。これまでに分かっている火星はどのような惑星なのだろうか。

Vocabulary Preview

Match each word with a definition by drawing a line between them.

1. fascinated
2. telescope
3. accessible
4. celestial body
5. canyon
6. evidence
7. abundant
8. feature
9. collision
10. nuclear winter

- (a) in plentiful supply
- (b) extremely interested
- (c) a typical or important quality of something
- (d) something that we can see in the sky, such as the Sun or the stars
- (e) a deep valley with steep sides
- (f) an object containing lenses that you look through to see things that are far away
- (g) able to be reached
- (h) an accident in which something moving crashes into something else
- (i) reasons for believing something
- (j) a long period of cold and darkness that would occur after a nuclear war

 **Reading**

Humans have long been fascinated by the planet Mars, partly because it is visible from the Earth without using **advanced** telescopes. Its red color led to it being called the God of War in Roman **mythology** and associated with the Greek god **Ares**. As the name suggests, the month of March was named after Mars.

5   Apart from the Moon, which is the Earth's satellite and the most accessible celestial body for humans, Mars draws the most attention of politicians and astronomers, and will almost certainly be the first planet that humans visit. There are many factors that make the planet relatively attractive to us.

    Although Mars is only about half the size of the Earth, its days are almost the 10 same length, and its years are about twice as long. It is interesting to contrast this with other nearby planets: Mercury's days are **equivalent to** about 59 Earth days, while Venus's years are shorter than its days. Mars's gravity is only about 30 percent that of the Earth, but scientists think that it is probably **sufficient** for humans to adapt to.

15   Mars's atmosphere is very thin and does not appear to contain oxygen, but its **geology** is in some ways quite similar to that of the Earth, featuring polar ice caps, canyons, and volcanoes. It also has seasons and weather. Importantly, there is evidence that water exists as ice and in clouds, and possibly even in liquid form on the ground. It also appears that, in the past, there was abundant liquid water, leading 20 to speculation that the planet may have had life in the past and could support it in the future.

    Another attractive feature of Mars is its average distance from the Earth. Although it is not as close as Venus — which is extremely hot and probably impossible for a human to visit — it is, at about 78 million kilometers, closer than 25 Mercury, which is about 100 million kilometers away. Moving further away in the Solar System, Jupiter is about 628 million kilometers away. Whereas a trip to Mars typically takes between five and 10 months, a trip to Jupiter would generally take four or more years.

    Futurists like **Michio Kaku** believe that it is essential for humans to build 30 permanent colonies on Mars as an **insurance policy** in case of an **extinction-level event** on the Earth. Such an event could be the collision of the Earth with a large asteroid, as is thought to have caused the extinction of the dinosaurs, or a **manmade** disaster such as nuclear winter or very severe climate change.

Although official organizations like NASA are currently focused on unmanned exploration of Mars, initiatives like Mars One are actively planning for missions to 35 the planet bearing humans who plan to stay there permanently.

NOTES

advanced 最新の **mythology** 神話 **Ares** アレス（ゼウスとヘラの子、ローマ神話のマーズ）
equivalent to 〜と等しい **sufficient** 十分な **geology** 地質 **Michio Kaku**（加來 道雄）日系３世米国人の理論物理学者であり、米国では未来学者としても知られている **insurance policy**
保険証書 **extinction-level event** 地球壊滅的事件 **manmade** 人為的な

Comprehension Check

Choose the most suitable answer for each question.

1. What is the association of Mars with war?
   (a) Wars often occur in March.
   (b) It is similar to Jupiter.
   (c) The color of the planet led the Romans to associate the planet with war.

2. Which of the following is NOT a similarity between Mars and the Earth?
   (a) The length of the day
   (b) The atmosphere
   (c) The geology

3. What is said about the distance of Mars from the Earth?
   (a) It is closer than Mercury or Jupiter.
   (b) It has not yet been measured.
   (c) It is about the same distance as Venus.

4. What is a possible reason to build settlements on Mars?
   (a) It may be a more pleasant place to live than the Earth.
   (b) If the dinosaurs came back, we could run away to Mars.
   (c) We could move there if the Earth could no longer support life.

Best Summary ➤

....

From these four sentences, choose the one that summarizes the passage best.

1. Although humans have always been interested in Mars, it will never be possible to send people there.

2. Although sending humans to Mars is difficult, it is the most promising of all the planets in the Solar System.

3. Michio Kaku is a famous futurologist who believes that we should build colonies on Mars.

4. Mars is almost the same as the Earth, so it is likely to be a good place for humans to live.

Word Choice ➤

....

Choose a suitable expression to fill each blank.

1. The size of Mars is about half _____ the Earth.
   (a) belonging　　(b) which　　　　(c) that of　　　(d) than

2. Some futurists are _____ the possibility of a catastrophic event on the Earth.
   (a) hoping to　　(b) focused on　　(c) dedicated　　(d) working hard

3. Because interplanetary travel takes so long, those who go to Mars should be prepared for a _____ stay.
   (a) permanent　　(b) permanently　　(c) short　　　(d) temporary

4. One Mars year is roughly _____ two Earth years.
   (a) equivalent to　(b) the equivalence of　(c) same as　(d) as same as

5. The atmosphere on the Moon is too thin _____.
   (a) for humans to breath　　　　　(b) for humans breathing
   (c) for human breath　　　　　　(d) for humans to breathe

Composition ➤

....

Rearrange the words within the parentheses to make sentences.

1. 木星の公転周期（太陽を 1 周する時間）は地球の公転周期のほぼ 12 倍の長さである。
   The Jovian year (almost / as / as / is / long / times / twelve) the terrestrial year.

_____

2. 6月はローマ神話の女神であるジュノーにちなんで名づけられたと言われている。

The month of June (after / been / have / is / named / said / to) the Roman goddess Juno.

_____

3. 可能性は低いが、各国政府はもし大きな小惑星が地球に衝突したらどうするかを検討しなければならない。

Although it is unlikely, governments have to (case / consider / do / in / of / to / what) a large asteroid colliding with the Earth.

_____

4. 昔は、液体の水が火星の表面に存在していたと考えられる。

In the past, (existed / have / is / liquid / on / thought / to / water) the surface of Mars.

_____

Partial Dictation and Conversation

🎵 2-63

Listen to the dialogue, and fill in the missing words. Then, speak the dialogue with a partner. After speaking once or twice, switch roles.

A: Did you learn much about ⓵ _____ in school?

B: Well, ⓶ _____, I guess. We memorized the names of all the planets.

A: Is there anything else that ⓷ _____?

B: Well, the rings of Jupiter. I was also into science fiction, so I may have read about them in novels, too. And I remember that — apart from Mercury, Venus, and Mars — the planets are all very far away. The science fiction I read always assumed lightspeed travel, so that people could get around the planets ⓸ _____.

A: Oh, yeah, that's true. I wonder ⓹ _____.

Active Learning

Look at the Solar System data shown in the table below. Talk about the data with a partner, including the following questions.

1. Which planets are closest to and furthest from the Earth?

2. How do other planets compare to the Earth in terms of gravity?

3. How do other planets compare to the Earth in terms of size?

	Equatorial diameter (km)	Gravity (Earth=1)	Distance from Earth (max, million km)	Distance from Earth (min, million km)
Mercury	4,879	0.38	136	50
Venus	12,104	0.9	161	25
Earth	12,756	1	0	0
Mars	6,794	0.38	248	35
Jupiter	142,980	2.53	600	367
Saturn	1,120,540	0.44	1,028	744
Uranus	51,120	0.72	1,960	1,606
Neptune	49,530	1.14	2,910	2,677

[Data source: http://www.astromax.org/planets.htm]

 WORDS & PHRASES

Only Jupiter has a gravity much greater than that of the Earth. The other planets' gravities are similar to or lower (than that of the Earth).

Neptune, Uranus, Saturn, (and Jupiter) are very far _____.

Jupiter and Saturn are much bigger _____.

UNIT 20

Casting a Shadow

ブラックホールの神秘

ブラックホールは文字通り黒い穴と思われがちだが、極めて高密度で強い重力のため物質だけでなく光さえも逃れることができない天体である。その画像が世界各国の望遠鏡を連結させることによって捉えられた。

Vocabulary Preview

Match each word with a definition by drawing a line between them.

1. galaxy
2. observer
3. infinitesimal
4. remote
5. virtual
6. scan
7. immense
8. algorithm
9. surround
10. physicist

- (a) existing in a computer, for example, but not in physical form
- (b) rules for doing calculations or solving problems
- (c) a large group of stars and planets
- (d) a scientist who does research in physics
- (e) a person who watches something
- (f) to be located on all sides or all around something
- (g) extremely large
- (h) to examine an area carefully
- (i) far from cities and other places where many people live
- (j) infinitely small, slow, light, etc.

Contrary to what the name may suggest, black holes are not empty but actually contain a very large amount of matter that is highly **compressed**. That results in the black hole having a very strong gravitational pull, and nothing — not even light — can escape, **hence** the name.

5   The possibility of the existence of such **astronomical** objects was first considered in the 18th century, but it was not until 1958 that David Finkelstein defined the "**event horizon**," the point beyond which, approaching a black hole, an object could not escape. Scientists gradually came to realize that black holes are of prime importance, both for their physical characteristics and in understanding the universe. They are
10   thought to exist at the center of most galaxies and to bend **spacetime** itself, in such a way that, as an object approaches a black hole, it appears to an outside observer to slow to infinitesimal speed. It was also **determined** in the 1970s that black holes emit what is known as **Hawking radiation**, making it possible to detect them. In addition, hot gases and dust around a black hole emit light, and a black hole casts
15   a shadow against that light, meaning that it also ought to be possible to see a black hole.

The possibility of the existence of such objects was first considered in the 18th century, Black holes have captured the popular imagination for such a long time that it is easy to forget that we had never seen one until April, 2019.

Starting work more than a decade ago, scientists set up what they called the Event
20   Horizon Telescope Array, a network of eight linked telescopes in remote locations around the world, to form a planet-sized virtual telescope that can produce very **high-resolution** images. They pointed the telescopes toward the Messier 87 galaxy, 55 million light years from the Earth, and scanned it for 10 days. The amount of data captured was too immense to send over the Internet, so they saved it all to hard
25   drives which were flown to data processing centers. A student at **MIT** developed an algorithm to **piece together** the data from the telescopes into one image.

The result of their work is a stunning image — the first ever taken — of a **supermassive** black hole, surrounded by a ring of fire, with a mass 6.5 billion times that of our sun and much larger than our whole Solar System. It is thought to be one
30   of the biggest black holes in existence. The physicists were excited to see that the image matches what they had imagined.

The scientists involved say that this work has started a whole new field of research, and researchers will take and study similar images of other black holes, looking for **confirmation** and **refinement** of their theories on the nature of the universe.

35

NOTES

contrary to ～に反して   **compressed** 圧縮された   **hence** このような訳で   **astronomical** 天文の   **event horizon** 事象の地平線   **spacetime** 時空   **determine** ～を究明する   **Hawking radiation** ホーキング放射   **high-resolution** 解像度の高い   **MIT** = (Massachusetts Institute of Technology) マサチューセッツ工科大学   **piece together** ～をつなぎ合わせる   **supermassive** 超大質量の   **confirmation** 確認   **refinement** 改善

Comprehension Check

Choose the most suitable answer for each question.

1. What do black holes contain?
   (a) They are empty.
   (b) They contain compressed matter.
   (c) They contain one or more event horizons.

2. How common are black holes?
   (a) There is believed to be one black hole in the universe.
   (b) There is believed to be one black hole in most galaxies.
   (c) There is believed to be one black hole in most Solar Systems.

3. Which of the following statements is NOT true of the Event Horizon Telescope Array?
   (a) The telescopes are located in another galaxy.
   (b) It consists of eight telescopes.
   (c) Together, the telescopes collected a very large amount of data.

4. Why is the black hole interesting theoretically?
   (a) It confirms what physicists believed about black holes.
   (b) It is just like the other black holes that physicists have discovered.
   (c) It is much smaller than expected.

Best Summary

From these four sentences, choose the one that summarizes the passage best.

1. Scientists have recently discovered that black holes have much stronger gravity than was originally believed.

2. David Finkelstein's theories, having been disputed for some time, have now been proven correct.

3. Using a network of telescopes, a team of scientists have created and shown the first ever image of a black hole.

4. Scientists have shown that working hard for a long time can lead to major discoveries.

Word Choice

Choose a suitable expression to fill each blank.

1. It was _____ 2019 that we actually saw a black hole.
   (a) until   (b) within   (c) not until   (d) yet

2. An MIT student was one of the people _____ in getting a picture of a black hole.
   (a) responsive   (b) guilty   (c) implicated   (d) involved

3. Black holes are _____ one of the keys to understanding the universe.
   (a) considered being   (b) thought to be   (c) deemed to have   (d) recognized to

4. _____ of telescopes can be more powerful than a single telescope.
   (a) A vision   (b) An array   (c) A sequence   (d) Multiple

5. Scientists have gradually _____ realize that large-scale collaborations are the way to achieve great things.
   (a) became   (b) came to the   (c) come to   (d) became to

Composition

Rearrange the words within the parentheses to make sentences.

1. イベント・ホライズン・テレスコープ配列はとても強力な装置なので、遠方の銀河系ですら解像度の高い画像を捉えることができる。

   The Event Horizon Telescope Array (a / can / device / is / it / powerful / such / that) capture high-resolution images even of faraway galaxies.

   _____

2. 科学者たちが「ホーキング放射」と呼ばれるものを発見したのは 1970 年代だ。

It was (called / discovered / in / scientists / that / they / what)
"Hawking radiation."

_____

3. 私たちの多くが学校で学んだことに反して、ブラックホールは何かを放射するが、このことがホーキング放射である。

Contrary (in / learned / many / of / school / to / us / what), black holes
do emit something: Hawking radiation.

_____

4. テキサスのホビー・エバリー望遠鏡は現存する一番大きな望遠鏡の一つである。

The Hobby-Eberly Telescope in Texas (existence / in / is / largest / of / one /
telescopes / the).

_____

Partial Dictation and Conversation

Listen to the dialogue, and fill in the missing words. Then, speak the dialogue with a
partner. After speaking once or twice, switch roles.

A: Do you understand black holes?

B: Not really. [1] _____. But I know that it's an area
of space with highly compressed matter. And I've heard that nothing can
escape a black hole.

A: But [2] _____. Didn't physicists show us an
image of a black hole in 2019? If even light can't escape, how could we see a
black hole?

B: Well, we can't actually see [3] _____. The black
hole casts a shadow over the light from the hot gases that are around the black
hole.

A: Oh, I see. So, [4] _____ to visit a black hole
anytime soon?

B: I think I'll [5] _____ on that! But if you're
interested, be my guest!

Active Learning

Look at the timeline below, which shows selected events in black hole science. Talk about this history with a partner, including the following questions.

1. When did Einstein predict the existence of black holes?

2. What happened in 1967?

3. What significant things have happened in the last 10 years?

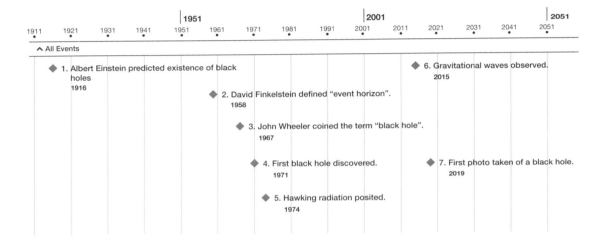

[Data sources: https://www.space.com/15421-black-holes-facts-formation-discovery-sdcmp.html
https://en.wikipedia.org/wiki/Black_hole]

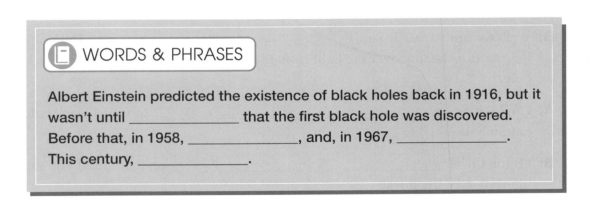

WORDS & PHRASES

Albert Einstein predicted the existence of black holes back in 1916, but it wasn't until _____ that the first black hole was discovered. Before that, in 1958, _____, and, in 1967, _____. This century, _____.

TEXT PRODUCTION STAFF

edited by Yasutaka Sano Masato Kogame	編集 佐野 泰孝 小亀 正人
English-language editing by Bill Benfield	英文校閲 ビル・ベンフィールド
cover design by Nobuyoshi Fujino	表紙デザイン 藤野 伸芳
text design by Ruben Frosali	本文デザイン ルーベン・フロサリ

CD PRODUCTION STAFF

recorded by Howard Colefield (AmerE) Rachel Walzer (AmerE)	吹き込み者 ハワード・コルフィールド（アメリカ英語） レイチェル・ワルザー（アメリカ英語）

Science Quest
未来科学への誘い

2020年1月20日　初版発行
2024年3月5日　第6刷発行

著　者　安浪 誠祐
　　　　Richard S. Lavin

発行者　佐野 英一郎

発行所　株式会社 成美堂
　　　　〒101-0052　東京都千代田区神田小川町3-22
　　　　TEL 03-3291-2261　FAX 03-3293-5490
　　　　https://www.seibido.co.jp

印刷・製本　三美印刷（株）

ISBN 978-4-7919-7205-0　　　　　　　　　　　Printed in Japan